# Bible Fun Stuff

## FOR AGES 2-5

# 100's of Songs, Games, and More!

FOR AGES 2-5

# 100's of Songs, Games, and More!

100'S OF SONGS, GAMES, AND MORE!
Published by David C. Cook
4050 Lee Vance View
Colorado Springs, CO 80918 USA

David C. Cook Distribution Canada
55 Woodslee Avenue, Paris, Ontario, Canada N3L 3E5

David C. Cook U.K., Kingsway Communications
Eastbourne, East Sussex BN23 6NT, England

David C. Cook and the graphic circle C logo
are registered trademarks of Cook Communications Ministries.

Editorial Manager: Doug Schmidt
Project Developer: Karen Pickering
Edited by: Dave and Neta Jackson
Designed by: Mike Riester
Illustrations by: Aline Heiser

ISBN 978-0-7814-3966-4

First Printing 2003
Printed in the United States of America

5 6 7 8 9 10 11 12 13 14

050109

# Thank You

for your help in this project:

Penny Anderson
Chris Behnke
Deborah Berkimer
Karen Brigham
Nancy Brown
Edna Mae Busch
Robin Currie
Anna Marie Dahiquist
Jeanette Dali
Betty Free
Christine French
Marilyn Hailman
Carl Heine
Amy and Rebekah Hill
Neta Jackson
Carolyn Joyce
Lois Keffer
Debbie Powell
Donald and Brenda Rateliff
Laurie Riddle
Janet Southern
Susan Stegenga
Judy Stonecipher
Beth Swale
Anna Trimiew
Tamara Valine
Ramona Warren

# Contents

# 100 Toddler Action Songs

We've selected rhymes and actions appropriate for toddlers. A few simple, familiar tunes have been used over and over so that two and three year olds can easily grasp the meaning of the words.

—The editors

## Songs About Jesus and God

**1** Help toddlers praise God by singing these words to the tune, *Row, Row, Row Your Boat*.

**Worship God today,**
**Worship with a clap.**
    Clap hands on the word clap
**Joyfully, joyfully, joyfully, joyfully,**
    Clap hands in rhythm
**Worship with a clap.**
    Clap hands on the word clap

**2** This rhyme, to the tune *Farmer in the Dell*, will help toddlers learn about God's creation.

**First a flower is small;**
    Crouch low
**Then it grows so tall.**
    Stand tall and stretch arms up
**I like flowers big and small.**
    Stand tall, then crouch low
**I'm glad God made them all.**
    Stand and clap hands

**3** Let children pretend to swim or fly as you sing the following song to the tune of *Row, Row, Row Your Boat*.

**Splish, splash, splish and splash.**
**Fish go swimming by.**
**God made fish both big and small,**
**They swim all day and night.**
**Flip, flap, flip and flap.**
**Birds go flying by.**
**God made birds both big and small,**
**They fly high in the sky.**

**4** Sing these words to the tune, *Old MacDonald Had a Farm* as children hold hands and walk in a circle changing directions on each verse.

**God made horses, sheep, and cows.**
**Neigh, neigh, baa, baa, moo.**
**The farmer cares for each of them.**
**God shows him what to do.**
**Farmers feed the animals hay.**
**Yum, yum, that tastes good.**
**God helps farmers grow the hay.**
**Because it is good food.**
**God made all the noisy squirrels.**
**Chatter, chee-chee, chee.**
**God made acorns, leaves, and nuts**
**For the squirrels to eat.**

**5** Sing this "story" about Zacchaeus to the tune of *Are You Sleeping?*

**Where's Zacchaeus, where's Zacchaeus?**
    Look around
**In a tree, in a tree,**
    Point up
**Waiting to see Jesus, waiting to see Jesus.**
    Shield eyes with hand
**In a tree, in a tree.**
    Point up
**Here comes Jesus, here comes Jesus.**
    Have fingers of right hand "walk"
    on left arm
**Down the road, down the road.**
**Jesus sees Zacchaeus, Jesus sees Zacchaeus.**
    Shield eyes with hand

*(Continued on next page.)*

5

In a tree, in a tree.
> Point up

Jesus told him, Jesus told him
To come down, to come down.
> Motion to come

Jesus helped Zacchaeus, Jesus helped
Zacchaeus
Do what's right, do what's right.
> Clap hands

**6** Sing these words to the tune of
*The Farmer in the Dell.*

God loves us-it's true.
> Point to self

God loves us-it's true.
We can thank God for His love.
> Spread arms wide

God loves us-it's true.
> Point to self

Noah built an ark.
> Pretend to use hammer or saw

Noah built an ark.
Noah did what God told him.
> Cup hand behind ear.

Noah built an ark.
> Pretend to use hammer or saw

Moses crossed the Sea.
> March in place

Moses crossed the Sea.
Moses knew that God would help.
> Spread arms wide

Moses crossed the sea.
> March in place

Elijah got some food.
> Pretend to eat

Elijah got some food.
Elijah thanked God for His love.
> Pretend to pray

Elijah got some food.
> Pretend to eat

**7** Teach this to the tune of *Mary Had a Little
Lamb.* Have toddlers clap their hands
every time they say the word, "Clap."

Show you love God with a clap,
With a clap, with a clap.
Show you love God with a clap,
Clap and clap and clap!

**8** Sing this action rhyme to the tune of
*Are You Sleeping?*

Who is Jesus? Who is Jesus?
> Shrug shoulders

He's God's Son. He's God's Son.
> Point up

Jesus is my Savior! Jesus is my Savior!
> Clap hands

He loves me! He loves me! Hug self

**9** This song, to *The Farmer in the Dell,* will
help toddlers learn to worship God.

I love God every day.
> Hug self

I love God every day.
> Hug self

I tell Him so each time I pray.
> Fold hands

I love God every day.
> Hug self

**10** Help toddlers praise and worship God by
singing these words to the tune of *Are
You Sleeping?*

Who made mountains?
> Touch fingertips to make mountain

Who made sunshine?
> Touch fingertips overhead

Who made birds?
> Wave arms

Flying free?
> Turn in a circle while waving arms

Who made all the spiders?
> Wiggle fingers of one hand on other arm

Who made all the flowers?
> Cup hands with wrists together

God made them.
> Spread arms wide

He loves me.   Hug self

**11** Clap in rhythm as you sing these words to *Mary Had a Little Lamb*. Add more verses by replacing "morning" with other things God has made such as evening, water, animals, people, and friends.

**Clap your hands and sing a song,**
**Sing a song, sing a song.**
**Clap your hands and sing a song:**
**Thank You, God, for morning!**

**12** Use these words and actions to the tune of *London Bridge Is Falling Down*.

**Who made the sun to light the day?**
   Touch fingertips overhead
**God did! God did!**
**God made the sun to light the day.**
   Touch fingertips overhead
**Thank You, God.**
**Who made stars that shine all night?**
   Wiggle fingers in the air
**God did! God did!**
**God made stars that shine all night.**
   Wiggle fingers in the air
**Thank You, God.**
**Who made fish and birds that fly?**
   Put palms together and swish,
   flap arms
**God did! God did!**
**God made fish and birds that fly.**
   Put palms together and swish,
   flap arms
**Thank You, God.**
**Who made grass and trees so tall?**
   Wave arms in air
**God did! God did!**
**God made grass and trees so tall.**
   Wave arms in air
**Thank You, God.**
**Who made dogs to run and play?**
   Tap hands on knees
**God did! God did!**
**God made dogs to run and play.**
   Tap hands on knees
**Thank You, God.**

**13** Have children clap as they thank God by singing this song to *Old MacDonald Had a Farm*.

**God can hear me when I sing.**
**Joyfully, I say, "Thank You,**
**thank You, thank You, God,**
**For Your love today."**

**14** Teach toddlers about Jesus' love by singing these words to *London Bridge Is Falling Down*.

**Jesus loves me very much,**
   Hug self
**Very much, very much.**
**Jesus loves me very much,**
   Hug self
**He's my friend.**
   Clap hands

**15** Talk to toddlers explaining that God hears us pray to Him no matter what we are doing. Then sing these words to the tune, *The Farmer in the Dell*.

**When I hurt my knee**
   Rub knee
**I can talk to God.**
   Fold hands to pray
**God listens when I pray to Him;**
   Cup hand to ear
**I can talk to God.**
   Fold hands to pray
Additional verses (add your own actions):
• **When I'm sick in bed**
• **When I'm feeling sad**
• **When I go to church**
• **When I go to sleep**
• **When I'm getting dressed**
• **When I'm eating lunch**
• **When I'm working hard**
• **When I lose my shoes**
• **When I help my dad**
• **When I'm having fun**
• **When I take a bath**

**16** Sing these words to the tune of *Jesus Loves Me*. Have children clap or use rhythm instruments as they sing.

Little children sang for Him,
Sang for Jesus long ago.
I will sing a song for Him,
For I know He loves me so.

I know He loves me,
And I love Him, too.
Jesus, hear me sing,
My songs of praise to You!

**17** Help toddlers learn about God by singing this to *Farmer in the Dell*.

God, You're very great!
   Spread arms wide
You made the little bee!
   Wiggle fingers by ear
You made the sun to shine for us.
   Touch fingers overhead
I'm glad that You made me!
   Point to self

**18** Teach toddlers to thank God as they sing this to the tune *Jesus Loves Me*.

Thank You, God, for everything.
   Stretch arms wide
You're so very good to me!
   Point to self
Thank You, God, for all You do;
   Sweep arm to the right
Really, really! love You!
   Hug self; then point up
Yes, God, I love You.
Yes, God, I love You.
Yes, God, I love You.
I really do love You.

**19** Teach this song about what Jesus taught to the tune, *Row, Row, Row Your Boat*.

Jesus teaches us
   Point up then to self
About God's love and care.

I can clap my hands and know
   Clap hands
That God is always there.
Jesus teaches us
   Point up, then to self
About God's love and care.
I can reach up high and know
   Stretch up high
That God is always there.
Jesus teaches us
   Point up, then to self
About God's love and care.
I can fold my hands and know
   Fold hands as if to pray
That God is always there.
Jesus teaches us
   Point up, then to self
About God's love and care.
I can give a hug and know
   Hug self
That God is always there.

**20** Have children walk in a circle and clap as you sing these words to the tune *Farmer in the Dell*.

I'm glad God gives to me
A home where I can play.
I'll thank Him for my family,
That cares for me each day.

I'm glad God gives to me
Good food to eat each day.
I'll thank Him for the gifts He gives
Each time I start to pray.

**21** Have toddlers clap in rhythm as they sing these words to *Mary Had a Little Lamb*.

Talk to God at night and say,
"Thank You for a happy day."
When you wake in morning light,
Thank Him for a restful night.

**22** These words can be sung to the tune of *Mulberry Bush*.

Jesus always did good things,
　　March in place
Did good things, did good things.
Jesus always did good things,
He taught His friends to pray.
　　Fold hands
Jesus made sick people well,
　　Reach up and stretch
People well, people well.
Jesus made sick people well,
And helped them to obey.
　　Hold hands out, palms up
Here are other verses you could use:
• Jesus helped the blind man see.
• Jesus helped the lame man walk.


**23** This action song to *Mary Had a Little Lamb*, teaches children things they can do for God.

I love You! Yes, I love You!
　　Hug self, then point up
That is why I like to pray.
　　Fold hands; bow head
I love You! Yes, I love You!
I pray to God each day!
I praise You! Yes, I praise You!
　　Clap throughout this verse
That is why I like to sing.
I praise You! Yes, I praise You!
My praise to God I bring.
I thank You! Yes, I thank You!
　　Nod head
That is why I like to give.
　　Pretend to give an offering
I thank You! Yes, I thank You!
Everyday I live!

## Songs about You and Me

**24** Talk about all the things God cares for after you sing this to the tune *Skip to My Lou*.

Flowers grow in the rain and sun,
　　Squat down; then slowly stand
Birds build nests in the trees, they do.
　　Flap arms like a bird
God takes care of all of these.
　　Clap hands
He takes care of me, too.
　　Point to self.
God made animals, big and small,
　　Spread arms wide; then bring together
Fish that swim in the sea-it's true!
　　Make swimming motion
God takes care of all of these.
　　Clap hands
He takes care of me, too.
　　Point to self.


**25** Have children walk in a circle while singing these words to the tune of *London Bridge Is Falling Down*.

Jesus cares about His friends,
Young and old, big and small.
You are one of Jesus' friends!
Jesus loves you.


**26** Sing these words to the tune, *Mulberry Bush*. Have toddlers use rhythm instruments as they they sing.

Jesus is a friend of mine,
He is with me all the time.
Inside, outside, near, or far,
He is near wherever we are.

**27** Sing these words to *Happy Birthday* as children walk in a circle.

God gives us good rules,
That He'll help us obey.
Then we can be happy
At work and at play.

**28** Sing these words to the tune, *London Bridge Is Falling Down*.

God is with me when I jump,
Jump on the word jump
When I jump, when I jump.
God is with me when I jump,
God is good!
Clap hands

Here are other verses you can use, or think of your own:

• God is with me when I sleep.
Rest head on folded hands
• God is with me when I eat.
Pretend to eat

**29** Sing this action rhyme is to the tune of *Mulberry Bush*.

I have clothes that I can zip,
Pretend to zip jacket
I can zip, I can zip.
I am warm as I can be
God cares for me.
Point to self
I like ice cream I can lick,
Pretend to lick ice cream cone
I can lick, I can lick
Two big scoops-oh boy, yippee!
God cares for me.
Point to self.
God gave me a family,
Clap hands
Family, family.
I'm glad He did that for you see
God cares for me.
Point to self

**30** Sing this action rhyme to *Twinkle, Twinkle Little Star*.

God made Adam; God made Eve.
He made the first family.
God made you; God made me!
Point to group, point to self
God made everyone we see.
God made every part of me,
Point to self
My ears to hear; my eyes to see.
Point to ears; point to eyes

**31** Teach children this song to the tune of *Happy Birthday*.

I know Jesus loves you.
Point to friend
I know Jesus loves me.
Point to self
We all love one another
Hug self
In God's family.
Join hands to form circle

**32** Have children clap their hands as they sing these words to *Farmer in the Dell*.

I'm Jesus' special friend.
I'm Jesus' special friend.
He helps me know what's right to do.
I'm Jesus' special friend!

**33** Sing this rhyme to *Mulberry Bush* as toddlers hold hands and walk in a circle.

You and I will be kind today,
Kind today, kind today.
You and I will be kind today,
To everyone we see.

Here are other verses you might use:

• You and I will say, "Hi" today.
• You and I will smile today.

**34** Use this action rhyme to teach toddlers that Jesus cares about them no matter how they feel. Sing it to *Mary Had a Little Lamb*.

**Jesus cares if you are sad,**
Make a sad face
**If you're big or if you're small.**
Stretch tall, then squat
**Jesus wants you to be happy.**
Clap hands
**He cares about us all.**
Spread arms wide

**35** This action rhyme about prayer is sung to *Farmer in the Dell*.

**I can talk to God,**
Point to self, then up
**I can talk to God,**
Point to self, then up
**God listens when I pray to Him,**
Point up, then fold hands in prayer
**I can talk to God.**
Point to self, then up

**36** Toddlers will enjoy clapping to this happy song as they sing it to the tune of *Did You Ever See a Lassie?*

**I'm so glad we have the Bible,**
**The Bible, the Bible.**
**I'm so glad we have the Bible**
**To learn of our friend.**

**Our friend's name is Jesus.**
**Our friend's name is Jesus.**
**I'm so glad we have the Bible**
**To learn of our friend.**

**37** This fun song, to the tune of *Ten Little Indians*, teaches about the love of Jesus.

**Listen! Listen! Jesus loves me.**
Point to ears; then to self
**Listen! Listen! Jesus loves you.**
Point to ears; then to others
**Let's go out and tell our friends**
Cup hands around mouth

**That Jesus loves us all!**
Hug self

**38** Sing these words to the tune, *Good Night, Ladies*. Have children point to the part of the body the song talks about (you can add other verses for knees, ears, feet, and so on), or have children do the actions the words tell them.

**Where is your nose?**
**Where is your nose?**
**Where is your nose?**
**Thank God for your nose.**
**Sit right down now.**
**Sit right down now.**
**Fold your hands now.**
**Thank God for everything.**

**39** Sing this action rhyme to the tune, *Mary Had a Little Lamb*. Talk to the children about how God cares for all that He has created.

**I'm a flower growing tall,**
Stoop down and rise slowly
**Growing tall, growing tall.**
**I'm a flower growing tall.**
**God takes care of me.**
Clap hands
**God will send the sunshine bright,**
Touch fingertips overhead
**Sunshine bright, sunshine bright.**
**God will send the sunshine bright.**
**God takes care of me.**
Clap hands
**I'm a bird that flies so high,**
Flap arms up and down
**Flies so high, flies so high.**
**I'm a bird that flies so high.**
**God takes care of me.**
Clap hands
**God gives twigs to build a nest,**
Cup hands to form a nest
**Build a nest, build a nest.**
**God gives twigs to build a nest.**
**God takes care of me.**
Clap hands

**40** Here's another rhyme about God's care for us. Sing it to the tune, *Farmer in the Dell.*

**God gives the birds their food.**
Flap arms up and down
**God gives the birds their food.**
**But God loves me much more than these.**
**He takes good care of me!**
**God makes the flowers grow.**
Stoop down and rise slowly
**God makes the flowers grow.**
**But God loves me much more than these.**
**He takes good care of me!**

**41** Let toddlers hold hands and walk in a circle as they sing these words to the tune, *Farmer in the Dell.*

**God gives us food to eat,**
**God gives us food to eat.**
**He gives us farmers who can help.**
**God gives us food to eat.**

**God knows our every need,**
**God knows our every need.**
**He gives us people who can help.**
**God knows our every need.**

**42** Sing this action song to *London Bridge Falling Down.*

**God said we should work six days,**
Pretend to hammer
**Work six days, work six days.**
**He gives us rules to obey**
**Because He loves us.**
Hug self
**God said we should go to church,**
Walk in place
**Go to church, go to church.**
**He gives us rules to obey**
**Because He loves us.**
Hug self
**God said we should love each other,**
Put an arm around a friend
**Love each other, love each other.**
**He gives us rules to obey**

**Because He loves us**
Hug self

**43** Have children sing this action rhyme to the tune, *Row, Row, Row Your Boat.*

**I'm glad God made plants,**
**Pretty, pretty plants.**
**I'm glad God made the tall oak tree.**
Stretch arms high
**And that God made me.**
Point up, then to self
**I'm glad God made spring,**
**Pretty, pretty spring.**
**I'm glad God made the rain we see,**
Wiggle fingers like falling rain
**And that God made me.**
Point up, then to self
**I'm glad God made birds,**
**Pretty, pretty birds.**
Flap arms like wings
**I'm glad God made the bumblebee,**
Wiggle fingers near your face
**And that God made me.**
Point up, then to self

**44** This rhyme teaches toddlers to give thanks. Sing it to the tune, *London Bridge Is Falling Down.*

**I thank God for trees and flowers,**
Fold hands as if in prayer.
**Trees and flowers, trees and flowers.**
**I thank God for trees and flowers,**
**I know they come from You.**
Clap hands
Other verses:
• **I thank God for day and night.**
Point up to the sun; rest cheek on hands
• **I thank God for food I eat.**
Pretend to eat.

**45** Sing this fun song to the tune, *Twinkle, Twinkle Little Star*. Have children do what the words say.

Touch your knees
And touch your nose.
Touch your head
Then your toes.
Touch your stomach,
Touch your eye.
Bend down low,
Then reach up high.
Turn around,
And look and see
God made everyone
Wonderfully.

**46** Sing these words to the tune, *Mary Had a Little Lamb*. Have children walk around the room with a friend while singing this rhyme.

Who loves me when I am good?
God does! God does!
When I do the things I should,
Yes, God loves me!
Who loves me when I feel bad?
God does! God does!
Even though He, too, feels sad,
Yes, God loves me!
Every day, who cares for me?
God does! God does!
When I'm sad, as sad can be,
God cares for me!

**47** Sing this action rhyme to the tune, *Twinkle, Twinkle Little Star*.

Here're my hands to work for God.
> Hold out hands

Here're my ears and here're my eyes.
> Point to ears, then eyes

I want to watch and listen, too,
> Shape hands like binoculars,
> then cup them behind ears

For the jobs that are just my size.
Here're my hands to work for God.
> Hold out hands

Here're my ears and here're my eyes.
> Point to ears, then eyes

**48** Teach toddlers how specially God made them by singing these words to *Farmer in the Dell*.

God gave me legs to stand,
> Stand up

And arms so I can stretch.
> Stretch

God made me very specially.
> Point up, then to self

God made me.
> Point up, then to self

God gave me feet to run,
> Run in place

And hands so I can clap.
> Clap

God made me very specially.
> Point up, then to self

God made me.
> Point up, then to self

God gave me a head to nod,
> Nod

And eyes so I can blink.
> Shut, open eyes

God made me very specially.
> Point up, then to self

God made me.
> Point up, then to self

**49** This little rhyme, to the tune *Mulberry Bush*, teaches children about praying.

When I pray, I talk to God,
> Fold hands in prayer

Talk to God, talk to God.
God hears everything I say
> Cup hand behind ear

When I talk to Him.
> Fold hands in prayer

## Songs about Family and Friends

**50** Sing this short little rhyme to the tune, *Twinkle, Twinkle Little Star.*

God cares for me
While I'm small,
  Bend low
Just as He will
When I'm tall.
  Stand tall

**51** Teach toddlers this action rhyme to *Happy Birthday.*

My two ears can hear,
  Point to ears
My two eyes can see.
  Point to eyes
It's God who made us,
  Raise arms
Both you and me.
  Point to another, then to self

**52** Have children clap and walk in a circle as they sing these words to *The Farmer in the Dell.*

My parents help me grow.
My parents help me grow.
They give me love and food and clothes.
My parents help me grow.

My teacher helps me grow.
My teacher helps me grow.
She (He) helps me learn what I should know.
My teacher helps me grow.

God helps us all to grow.
God helps us all to grow.
He gives us everyone we need
To help us all to grow.

**53** Sing this action rhyme to the tune *Mary Had a Little Lamb.*

Baby elephant swings his trunk,
  Bend over, join hands for trunk
Like his father and his mother.
  Same action
God gave me a family, too,
  Point to self
And we love each other.
  Hug self

**54** Have children walk in a circle as they sing this to *Mulberry Bush.* Sing more verses by using names of other family members.

We can thank God for our moms
For our moms, for our moms.
We can thank God for our moms.
Thank You God.

**55** Have children do what this action song says as they sing it to the tune, *Are You Sleeping?*

Let's be friends. Let's be friends.
Clap with me. Clap with me.
Come and clap with me.
Come and clap with me.
Clap. Clap. Clap. Clap. Clap. Clap.

In place of *clap* use other action words such as hop, march, smile, and hug.

**56** Before you sing these words to the tune, *Farmer in the Dell*, talk with toddlers about ways they can show love to others. Do motions for their suggestions as you sing these words.

Now we can show our love.
Now we can show our love.
We show our love as Jesus did.
Now we can show our love.

**57** Sing these words to *Mulberry Bush* as you lead children in these actions.

Won't you come and march with me.
March with me, march with me?
Won't you come and march with me?
I'm glad that I can march.

Other verses could include the actions clap, jump, run, sit, or pray.

**58** Sing these words to the tune, *Row, Row, Row Your Boat.*

One friend and one friend,
    Hold up one finger on each hand
Together they do know
    Hold fingers together
That a friend always loves you,
    Hug self
For God has made them so!
    Stretch arms wide

**59** Have children hold hands with a friend and walk in a circle as they sing this rhyme to the tune, *Farmer in the Dell*.

Its good to have a friend.
It's good to have a friend.
Together we have lots of fun.
It's good to have a friend.

## Songs about Helping

**60** Teach children about helping by singing these words to the tune, *Mary Had a Little Lamb*. Think of other ways that toddlers can help such as pick up toys or set the table.

**I can help to feed my pets,**
 Pretend to set out bowl; pour food
**Feed my pets, feed my pets.**
**I can help to feed my pets;**
**I can help at home.**
 Clap hands and smile
**Helping makes me happy, yes!**
 Clap hands and smile
**Happy, yes; happy, yes!**
**Helping makes me happy, yes,**
**When I help at home!**
 Clap and smile

**61** Have toddlers march around the room as they sing these words to the tune of *Farmer in the Dell*.

**How can I be good?**
**How can I be good?**
**Jesus helps me every day.**
**He helps me to be good.**

**I can share my toys.**
**I can share my toys.**
**Jesus helps me every day.**
**He helps me to be good.**

**62** You can use this action rhyme to the tune, *Mulberry Bush* to help toddlers learn to dress themselves.

**This is the way we put on our boots,**
 Pretend to pull on boots
**Put on our boots, Put on our boots.**
**This is the way we put on our boots,**
**On a winter morning.**

Here are some additional verses you can use for the other seasons.

**This is the way we put up an umbrella**
 Pretend to put up an umbrella

**On a rainy, spring day.**
**This is the way we wear a sun hat**
 Pretend to put on a hat
**on a summer morning.**
**This is the way we put on a jacket**
 Pretend to put on a jacket
**On a cool, fall morning.**

**63** Sing this fun action rhyme to the tune of *Mary Had a Little Lamb*.

**Pat the cat and puppy dog.**
 Stroke one hand on the back of the other
**Pick up things for your mother.**
 Bend down and touch floor
**Smile and wave "hello" to friends.**
 Smile and wave
**Be kind to one another.**
 Spread arms wide

**64** Toddlers will enjoy marching around the room with a friend as they sing these words to the tune, *Twinkle, Twinkle Little Star*.

**We want to be kind and good,**
**Just as Jesus says we should.**
**Loving others every day,**
**Helping them in some small way.**
**We want to be kind and good,**
**Just as Jesus says we should.**

**65** Use this simple song to the tune of *Mulberry Bush* when you want the children to prepare for different activities. Vary the verses as you wish.

**Let's all put our toys away,**
**Toys away, toys away.**
**We will talk and listen to stories.**
**Let's put our toys away.**

**Let's all put our toys away,**
**Toys away, toys away.**
**We have listened and talked and played.**
**And now it's time to go.**

**66** Use this action rhyme to tell toddlers when it's time to pick up, toys or follow some other instruction. Sing this rhyme to the tune, *Twinkle, Twinkle Little Star*.

Hurry, scurry, 1, 2, 3.
>    Clap as you sing the numbers
Listen, listen carefully.
Time to put toys back in place.
Then put on a happy face.
Listen, listen carefully,
>    Pause with hand cupped behind ear
Hurry, scurry, 1, 2, 3!
>    Clap as you sing the numbers

**67** Sing these words to the tune, *Are You Sleeping?* Use them to teach children by adding a motion at the end of the song such as a helping activity or stretching exercise.

I am growing, I am growing,
Wise and tall, wise and tall.
See what I can do now.
See what I can do now.
Do it, too; do it, too.

**68** This rhyme is full of actions that will prepare children for a story, snack, or any listening time. Sing it slowly-so toddlers can follow the motions to the tune, *Ten Little Indians*.

Reach up high,
Then touch the ground.
Wave "hello,"
Then turn around.
Pat your head,
Then give a clap.
Sit right down with your
Hands in your lap.

**69** Here's another rhyme that helps prepare children to listen. Sing it to *Twinkle, Twinkle Little Star*.

Reach way up.
Then touch your toes,
Hands on shoulders,
Hands on nose.
Clap three times,
And turn around.
Fold your hands
And sit right down.
Now you're ready, 1, 2, 3,
'Cause It's time to listen to me.

**70** Here's the third rhyme you can use to get children's attention. Have them do what the words say as you sing the rhyme to the tune, *Are You Sleeping?*

Clap up high, clap up high.
Clap down low, clap down low.
Now clap in the middle,
Now clap in the middle
And down you go!
Down you go!
>    Sit with hands folded

**71** Use this song, to the tune of *Mulberry Bush*, to help toddlers get ready to listen to a story or special instructions.

Let's all play a listening game,
A listening game,
A listening game.
Let's all play a listening game,
Listen very closely.

## Songs about Church and Sunday School

**72** Sing this fun rhyme that helps young children learn about God's creation to the tune, *Mary Had a Little Lamb*.

**What kind of animal says, "Arf, arf"?**
**Says, "Arf, arf"? Says, "Arf, arf"?**
**What kind of animal says, "Arf, arf"?**
**Can you guess its name?**

**What kind of plant smells, oh, so nice?**
**Oh, so, nice? Oh, so nice?**
**What kind of plant smells, oh, so nice?**
**Can you guess its name?**

Here are some other ideas and actions for different animals:

- **What kind of animal says:**
  **"Moo, moo"?**
- **What kind of animal says:**
  **"Baa, baa"?**
- **What kind of animal says:**
  **"Oink, oink"?**
- **What kind of animal hops like this?**
  Hop like bunnies
- **What kind of animal walks like this?**
  Walk like dogs, ducks, and so forth

**73** This action rhyme, to the tune *Farmer in the Dell*, will teach children about worshiping together in church.

**Together we will pray**
  Fold hands in prayer
**And sing joyfully.**
  Clap hands two times
**We're glad that we are here in church**
  Point to selves
**With all God's family.**
  Spread arms wide

**74** Have children march around the room as they sing these words to the tune, *Mary Had a Little Lamb*. Don't forget to have them tell you their favorite thing to do.

**We like to come to Sunday school,**
**To learn and sing and to play.**
**What's your favorite thing to do**
**On this God's special day?**

**75** This song can be used to introduce the Bible story during Sunday school. Sing the words to the tune, *London Bridge Is Falling Down*. Use these words when telling the story of the miraculous catch of fish.

**We are going to catch some fish,**
**Catch some fish, Catch some fish.**
**We are going to catch some fish,**
**Catch some fish today.**

Try to think of words that would be suitable for other stories as well such as:

- **God told Noah to build an ark.**
- **David was a shepherd boy.**

**76** Sing these words about Sunday school. to *Farmer in the Dell*.

**At Sunday school, my friends**
  Hold hands
**And I learn how to pray.**
  Fold hands, bow head
**We're learning to love Jesus**
  Hug self
**And learning to obey.**
  Clap hands

**77** Have children sing these words to the tune of *Twinkle, Twinkle Little Star*.

**Church is such a happy place.**
  Clap hands
**See my smiling, happy face.**
  Smile
**It is where I laugh and sing**
  Skip in a circle
**And where I bring my offering.**
**Church is such a happy place.**
  Clap hands
**See my smiling, happy face.**
  Smile

**78** Teach children that God is a special friend by singing these words to the familiar tune of *Jesus Loves Me*. Have them play rhythm instruments as they sing.

**God's a special friend of mine.**
**He listens to me when I pray.**
**He wants us all to come to church**
**On this, His very special day.**

Refrain:

**God is my friend.**
**God is my friend.**
**God is my friend.**
**This Is His special day.**

**79** This is another song that you can make up lots of different verses as you sing it to the tune of *Farmer in the Dell* or *Row, Row, Row Your Boat*.

**We can sing at church.**

**We can sing at church.**
**Come along and join our song.**
**We can sing at church.**

**Who can beat the drum?**
**Who can beat the drum?**
**Come along and join our song!**
**Who can beat the drum?**
• **We can worship God.**
• **Who can clap their hands?**

**80** *Mary Had a Little Lamb* is a good melody to use to sing this action rhyme. These words help teach young children what to do at church.

**Let us sing our happiest songs.**
  Point to mouth
**Let us bring an offering to share.**
  Extend cupped hands
**Come and let us worship God**
  Beckon to children
**And thank Him with a prayer.**
  Fold hands

**81** Toddlers will enjoy this simple song to the tune of *London Bridge Is Falling Down*. Have them walk in a circle and clap their hands as they sing.

**Oh, we love to go to church,**
**Go to church, go to church.**
**Oh, we love to go to church.**
**To worship God.**

**82** These words, sung to *Mulberry Bush*, teach children what to do in church.

**This is the way we pray to God,**
  Fold hands; bow head
**Pray to God, pray to God.**
**This is the way we pray to God,**
**Each and every day.**
**This is the way we sing to God.**
  Pretend to look at a songbook
• **This is the way we give to God.**
  Pretend to give offering
• **This is the way we listen to stories.**
  Cup hands around ears

## Songs about Christmas

**83** Give toddlers bells to shake as they sing this Christmas rhyme to *Jingle Bells.*

Ring these bells.
Ring these bells.
Ring them loud and clear.
Jesus Christ is born today.
Let's ring the bells all year!

**84** Sing this simple action song to the tune of *Mulberry Bush.*

My face can smile; my hands can clap.
    Point to smile; then clap two times
My face can smile; my hands can clap.
My face can smile; my hands can clap.
I'm happy 'cause it's Christmas!
    Spread arms wide

**85** Sing these words slowly so toddlers can imitate the words and actions. Use the tune *Happy Birthday.*

A Savior's been born!
    Cup hands around mouth
Hurry up! We can run
    Run in place
To see baby Jesus.
    Circle eyes with fingers
God sent us His Son.
    Fold arms as if rocking baby

**86** Have toddlers march around the room clapping as they sing these words to the tune of *Skip to My Lou.*

We can praise Him with a clap.
We can praise Him with a clap.
We can praise Him with a clap.
God sent His Son Jesus.

**87** Even very young children will enjoy and understand this simple action song. Have them clap as they sing it to the tune, *Mulberry Bush.*

Sing a song and clap your hands.
Clap your hands, clap your hands.
Sing a song and clap your hands.
Happy birthday, Jesus!

**88** Sing these words to the tune, *The Farmer in the Dell.* If you wish, children could act out the verses as if they were putting on a Christmas play. You could even provide simple costumes. Have them clap as they sing the first verse; repeat that verse at the end as well.

Oh, happy Christmastime.
Oh, happy Christmastime.
We're glad that baby Jesus came
At happy Christmastime!

The cows and sheep were there.
The cows and sheep were there.
We're glad that baby Jesus came
At happy Christmastime!
The shepherds hear the news.
The shepherds hear the news.
We're glad that baby Jesus came
At happy Christmastime!

The Wise Men saw the star.
The Wise Men saw the star.
We're glad that baby Jesus came
At happy Christmastime!

**89** Sing this action rhyme to the tune of *Happy Birthday.*

Baby Jesus came to earth,
And He was very small.
    Pretend to hold baby
God sent us little Jesus
Because He loves us all!
    Point up, then hug self

**90** This action song can be sung to *Twinkle, Twinkle, Little Star.*

**Baby Jesus sleeping in the hay;**
    Rest your head on your hands
**Shepherds kneeling as they pray,**
    Kneel; fold hands in prayer
**Thanking God for sending His Son**
    Point up
**Thanking Him for all He's done.**
**Baby Jesus sleeping in the hay;**
    Rest your head on your hands
**On this special Christmas Day.**
    Clap hands

**91** Have children sing this song to the tune, *Mulberry Bush.*

**Mary rocks her baby boy,**
    Pretend to rock baby
**Baby boy, baby boy.**
**Then she lays Him down to sleep**
    Pretend to put baby down
    and go sh-h-h
**In a manger bed.**
**Animals and shepherds watch**
    Shield eyes with hands
**Little baby Jesus.**
**Lying there so quietly**
    Pretend to sleep: rest head on hands
**On His bed of hay.**

**92** To the tune of *Ten Little Indians*, sing the first verse softly, putting a finger to your lips when you say, "Sh." Sing the second verse loudly, clapping when you say, "Thanks."

**Sh! Sh! See the baby Jesus.**
**Sh! Sh! Sleeping on the hay.**
**Sh! Sh! See the baby Jesus.**
**Born on Christmas Day.**

**Thanks! Thanks! Thank You, God, for Jesus.**
**Thanks! Thanks! Thank You for Your Son.**
**Thanks! Thanks! Thank You, God, for Jesus.**
**Joy for everyone.**

**93** Have children walk in a circle as they sing these words to *London Bridge.*

**God loved us and sent His Son,**
**Sent His Son, sent His Son.**
**God loved us and sent His Son,**
**His Son Jesus.**

**94** Here's another simple Christmas action song that young children will enjoy. Sing it to the tune of *Skip to My Lou.*

**Hear the news the angels sing.**
    Point to ears
**Hear the news the angels sing.**
**Hear the news the angels sing.**
**God sent His Son, Jesus.**
    Clap hands
**Shepherds run to Bethlehem.**
    Run in place
**Shepherds run to Bethlehem.**
**Shepherds run to Bethlehem.**
**God sent His Son, Jesus.**
    Clap hands
**We can praise Him with a clap.**
    Clap hands throughout verse
**We can praise Him with a clap.**
**We can praise Him with a clap.**
**God sent His Son, Jesus.**

## Songs about Easter

**95** Let toddlers march around the room as they sing this happy song to the tune, *London Bridge Is Falling Down.*

Easter is a special time
So let's sing a happy song.
Alleluia! Alleluia!
You can sing along.

**96** Sing these words to the tune of *Are You Sleeping?*

Girls and boys, sing for joy.
  Cup hands around mouth
Easter day! Celebrate!
  Stretch out arms
Jesus is alive, Jesus is alive!
  Clap hands
Sing for joy, sing for joy.
  Cup hands around mouth

**97** Sing this action rhyme slowly so young children will be able to follow the words and motions. Use the tune, *Ten Little Indians.*

Clap your hands!
  Clap twice
The sun is shining.
  Touch fingertips overhead
Clap your hands
  Clap twice
And shout "Hooray!"
  Cup hands around mouth
Clap your hands,
  Clap twice
For Jesus loves us.
  Hug self
He's alive today!
  Squat down; then jump up on "alive"

**98** This action rhyme can be sung to the tune of *Mary Had a Little Lamb.*

Morning sun is shining bright.
  Touch fingertips overhead
Wear a smile this happy day!
  Point to smile
Clap your hands now, 1, 2, 3.
  Clap as you sing the numbers
Jesus is alive-hooray!
  Jump on the word "hooray"

**99** This song, to the tune of *Happy Birthday*, provides a good opportunity for toddlers to use rhythm instruments. Sing it through a couple of limes before they "play" their instruments.

I'm so glad for Easter.
It's such a special day!
Jesus came back to life,
He's alive today!

I'm so glad for Easter.
It's such a special day!
Let's tell the Good News
Jesus still lives today!

**100** After singing these words to the tune of *Mary Had a Little Lamb*, teach children that they talk to Jesus when they pray.

Jesus is my special friend.
  Skip in a circle
Special friend, special friend.
Jesus is my special friend,
And He's alive today.
  Clap hands
Jesus listens when I pray,
  Cup hand behind ear; then fold hands
When I pray, when I pray.
Jesus listens when I pray,
For He's alive today.
  Clap hands

# 100 More Toddler Action Songs

## Songs About Our World

**1** Sing these words to the tune of *Ring Around the Rosey* as children march in a circle. Then ask children to tell you some other things God made and make up as many verses as you'd like.

**God makes the rainbows.**
**God makes the rainbows.**
**Rainbows, rainbows.**
**Thank You, God.**

**2** Children will enjoy this simple song sung to the tune *Twinkle, Twinkle, Little Star.*

**Spring and summer, winter, fall.**
> Children clap on first two lines

**Thank You, God! You made them all.**
> Children point up for last two lines

**3** This next song tells of some other things God made. Use the tune of *Paw-Paw Patch.*

**God made fish. God made flowers.**
> Wiggle wrists with palms together, then sniff

**God made apples and rain showers.**
> Rub stomach, then wiggle fingers overhead

**God made mountains, stars, and trees**
> Touch fingertips overhead, wiggle fingers, then reach high

**Made them everyone for you and me!**
> Point to self

**4** For this song, sung to *Skip to My Lou,* have children hold hands and move around as they sing. On the last line have everybody stop and clap to the rhythm.

**Who made the hills and the stars at night?**
> Touch fingertips overhead; wiggle fingers in air

**Who made the grass and clouds so white?**
> Touch floor; wave arms overhead

**Who made the birds and giraffes so tall?**
**God is the One who made them!**
> Clap four times in rhythm

**5** Toddlers will love singing this song and choosing animals to sing about in each verse. As they sing the verses have them act out each animal named. Use the tune of *Old MacDonald Had a Farm.*

**I'm so glad God made the duck.**
**G-L-A-D glad!**
**I'm glad God gave him a home.**
**G-L-A-D glad!**
**With a quack, quack here**
**And a quack, quack there,**
**Here a quack, there a quack,**
**Everywhere a quack, quack.**
**I'm so glad God made the duck.**
**G-L-A-D glad.**

**6** Children will pretend to be little seeds as they do the actions in this next song sung to the tune of *Skip to My Lou.*

**Little seed is in the ground.**
> Crouch on ground

**Rain falls gently, gently down.**
> Wiggle fingers overhead

**First a shoot and then a bud.**
> Slowly raise arms overhead

**Then a pretty flower!**
> Circle face with hands

**7** Have children stand in a circle as they sing and do actions for this song sung to the tune of *This Old Man*.

**Animals, one by one,**
> Hold up one finger

**Birds are flying, having fun.**
> Flap arms

**Refrain: There's a moose with antlers,**
> Touch thumbs to head with palms spread

**And a mouse so small.**
> Cup hands

**It is God who made them all!**
> Spread arms wide

**Animals, two by two,**
> Hold up two fingers

**See the hopping kangaroos,**
> Hop

*(Refrain)*

**Animals, three by three,**
> Hold up three fingers

**Whales go swimming in the sea.**
> Palms together, wiggle wrists

*(Refrain)*

**Animals, four by four,**
> Hold up four fingers

**Kingly lions start to roar.**
> Roar

*(Refrain)*

**Animals, five by five,**
> Hold up five fingers

**Bees are buzzing by their hive.**
> Wiggle fingers by ear

*(Refrain)*

**8** Use this song to teach about the five senses and to help toddlers be thankful to God for the wonderful world He has made. Have children do the action mentioned in each verse. Sing to *The Farmer in the Dell*.

**When I sniff a flower, I say thanks to God.**
**He's the One who made It sweet.**
**I say thanks to God.**

**When I hear a bird, I say thanks to God.**
**He's the One who made It sing.**
**I say thanks to God.**

**When I eat a peach, I say thanks to God.**
**He's the One who made It juicy.**
**I say thanks to God.**

**When I pet my cat, I say thanks to God.**
**He's the One who made her soft.**
**I say thanks to God.**

**When I see the world, I say thanks to God.**
**He's the One who made it all.**
**I say thanks to God.**

## Songs About Jesus and God

**9** Sing these words to the tune of *Mary Had a Little Lamb*. After each time the verse is sung ask children to name something God has given them.

**Thank You, God, for giving me**
　　Point up, then to self
**Giving me, giving me,**
**Thank You, God, for giving me**
**Everything I need.**

**10** Teach these words to the tune of *Mary Had a Little Lamb* and do the actions mentioned.

**Sing a song and clap your hands.**
**Clap your hands, clap your hands.**
**Sing a song and clap your hands.**
**We're praising God today.**

vs. 2 **Sing a song and fold your hands...**

**11** Use these words sung to *The Farmer in the Dell* to teach children about thanking God. Have them fold their hands as they sing.

**We like to talk to God.** (Repeat)
**We like to thank Him for our food.**
**Thank You, thank You, God.**

**12** Children will enjoy marching as they sing this song to the tune of *The Mulberry Bush*.

**Give thanks to God for everything**
**For everything, for everything.**
**Give thanks to God for everything**
**Everything He gives us!**

**13** Have toddlers hold hands and walk in a circle as they sing these words to the tune of *Oh, Dear, What Can the Matter Be?*

**Jesus went around doing good.**
**Jesus went around doing good.**
**Jesus went around doing good,**
**And I can do good things, too.**

For more verses, substitute these lines:

2. **Jesus taught His friends how to pray**
3. **Jesus taught His friends about God.**
4. **Jesus forgave the people, too.**
5. **He made the sick people well.**

**14** Have children act out the verses to this next song which is sung to the tune of *Ten Little Indians*.

**I have a friend, His name is Jesus.**
**I have a friend, His name is Jesus.**
**I have a friend, His name is Jesus.**
**He is with me all day long.**

**He is with me when I wake up.**
**He is with me when I wake up.**
**He is with me when I wake up.**
**He is with me all day long.**

vs.3 **He is with me when I get dressed.**
vs.4 **He is with me when I eat breakfast.**
vs.5 **He is with me when I run fast.**
vs.6 **He is with me when I am sleeping.**

**15** Have toddlers clap as they sing these words to the tune of *Row, Row, Row Your Boat*.

**Praise, praise, praise the Lord**
**For He is our King.**
**We love Him so we give Him praise**
**For He is our King.**
vs. 2 **Thank, thank, thank the Lord.**
vs. 3 **Love, love, love the Lord.**

**16** Lead children in singing these words to the tune of *Yankee Doodle*.

**Who loves you and who loves me?**
> Point to a friend on "you" and to self on "me"

**Who loves everybody?**
> Spread arms out

**God loves you and God loves me.**
> Repeat first line motions

**We're all in one big family!**
> Spread arms out

**God is love, oh, yes, it's true.**
> Clap on these last four lines

**God loves everybody.**
**God is love, oh, yes, it's true.**
**Yes, God loves everybody.**

**17** Teach toddlers a new song about Jesus using the tune of *The B-I-B-L-E*.

**My J-E-S-U-S,**
> Point up

**Yes, He's the very best!**
> Nod head "yes"

**He died and rose for you and me.**
> Clap hands

**My J-E-S-U-S.**
> Point up

**18** Have toddlers hold hands with a friend and swing arms together as they sing these words to the tune *Did You Ever See a Lassie?*

**Did you know that Jesus loves you?**
**He loves you. He loves you.**
**Did you know that Jesus loves you?**
**He loves you and me.**
**So sing a glad song now**
**And clap both your hands now.**
**Did you know that Jesus loves you?**
**He loves you and me.**

**19** Have children march in a circle as they sing these words to the tune of *Row, Row, Row Your Boat.*

**God, God, God is love.**
**He's with us all day.**
**We can show we love God, too.**
**With worship and with praise.**

**God, God, God is love.**
**He is love we know.**
**He gives good things to you and me**
**To show He loves us so.**

**God, God, God is love.**
**He is love we know.**
**He gives good leaders as a way**
**To show He loves us so.**

**God, God, God is love.**
**He is love we know.**
**He gives good rules to you and me**
**To show He loves us so.**

**20** Teach this song to *Good Night, Ladies.*

**Baby Jesus,**
> Sing quietly

**Baby Jesus.**
> Sing louder

**Baby Jesus**
> Sing louder still

**Was born In Bethlehem.**
> Clap on beat

vs. 2 Jesus grew up ...
> He soon was strong and tall.

vs. 3 He helped others ...
> Yes, Jesus did good things.

vs. 4 I am growing ...
> And Jesus is my friend.

**21** Lead children in doing the motions to this next song sung to *The Mulberry Bush*.

Jesus was a tiny babe,
> Rock a pretend baby

Tiny babe, tiny babe.
Jesus was a tiny babe,
Just like you and me.
> Point to friend, then self

vs. 2 **God kept Jesus safe from harm...**
> **Just like you and me.**
> Cross arms across chest

vs. 3 **God helped Jesus grow and learn...**
> **Just like you and me.**
> Crouch; then stretch on tiptoes

**22** Children will enjoy singing this song to the tune *Are You Sleeping?* Have them act out the words.

Jesus sat upon a hill
With His friends, with His friends.
All the little children
Wanted to see Jesus.
So they ran, so they ran.

"Stop the children, stop the children,"
Said the men, said the men.
Jesus said, "I love them,
And I want to bless them.
Let them come. Let them come."

**23** Children will enjoy making up their own actions to these words to the tune of *London Bridge*.

Jesus came to see His friends,
See His friends, see His friends.
Jesus came to see His friends.
They were happy.

Martha baked a loaf of bread,
Loaf of bread, loaf of bread.
Martha baked a loaf of bread
Just for Jesus.

Mary listened carefully,
Carefully, carefully.
Mary listened carefully
Just to Jesus.

**24** Teach children about the Bible by singing this song to the tune of *Are You Sleeping?*

In my Bible, in my Bible,
> Open hands, palms up

God tells me, God tells me,
> Point to self

Jesus is my good friend,
Jesus is my good friend,
> Smile and nod

He loves me, He loves me.
> Hug self

**25** Let children clap their hands as they learn this song which is sung to the tune of *Three Blind Mice*.

Praise the Lord!
Praise the Lord!
Joyfully, joyfully.
Give thanks to God for the food we eat,
Our homes and our church and our families.
Praise God for giving us all that we need.
Praise the Lord!
Praise the Lord!

**26** Here's another song where children can act out the words of the song. Sing to *Here We Go Looby Loo*.

Let's make a joyful noise,
And clap our hands 1-2-3.
Let's make a joyful noise,
For Jesus loves both you and me.

Add more verses by changing the second line to "Let's march our feet 1-2-3," or "Let's jump up high 1-2-3."

## Songs About Bible Friends

**27** *London Bridge* is a fitting tune for this song about Joshua and the walls of Jericho. Have children do motions for each verse.

Joshua marched 'round the wall,
'Round the wall, 'round the wall.
Joshua marched 'round the wall
Seven times.

On the last time horns did blow,
Horns did blow, horns did blow.
On the last time horns did blow,
The wall came down.

People shouted, "Praise the Lord,
Praise the Lord, praise the Lord."
People shouted, "Praise the Lord,
For He is great and mighty."

**28** Teach these words to *Mary Had a Little Lamb.*

David was a little boy,
    Put hand out as if patting small child on head
Little boy, little boy.
David was a little boy,
Who watched his father's sheep.
    Shield eyes with hand as if watching sheep
David liked to sing to God,
    Spread arms out as if singing heartily
Sing to God, sing to God.
David liked to sing to God
Because he loved Him so.
    Hug self

**29** *Oh, Dear, What Can the Matter Be?* is an appropriate tune for these words about Daniel in the lion's den.

Daniel went in the lion's den. (Repeat 2x)
    Walk in place
All of his friends were so sad.
    Make a sad face
He prayed and God shut the lion's mouth.
(Repeat 2x)
    Put hands together as if praying then slap hands shut to represent lion

Daniel was happy indeed!
    Make happy face

**30** Children will be encouraged to be like Noah as they sing this song to *The Farmer in the Dell.*

Noah loved the Lord. (Repeat)
    Clap hands
Noah listened when God spoke.
    Put hand to ear
Noah loved the Lord.
God said, "Go build an ark." (Repeat)
    Point finger
Noah listened when God spoke.
    Put hand to ear
God said, "Go build an ark."
vs. 3 Noah built an ark
vs. 4 I'm like Noah, too...

**31** Have toddlers play rhythm instruments as they sing this next song to the tune of *Ten Little Indians.*

I may never preach like Moses.
I may never preach like Moses.
I may never preach like Moses,
But I love the Lord.
vs. 2 I may never build like Noah.
vs. 3 I may never rule like Joash.
vs. 4 I may never build like Nehemiah.

**32** This action song about Noah is sung to *Jesus Loves Me.*

Noah built a great big boat.
    Pretend to hammer
God told Him that it would float
    Make floating boat with hands
When the rains began to fall
    Make raining motion with fingers
God did save them one and all.
    Clap hands
Gather the animals.
    Children pretend to be their favorite animal
Gather the animals.
Gather the animals.
God saved them one and all.

**33** Have children do the motions as they sing this next song to the tune of *Oh, Be Careful.*

We can fold our hands like this when we pray.
We can fold our hands like this when we pray.
God will hear us when we pray.
He'll hear everything we say.
We can fold our hands like this when we pray.

For more verses, substitute these words for the first, second and last lines of the song.

We can hold each other's hands when we pray.
We can lift our hands up high when we pray.

**34** Children will enjoy doing motions for each verse of this song which is sung to *The Mulberry Bush.*

I can worship God today,
With my hands, with my hands.
When I clap my hands and sing,
I worship God this morning.

I can worship God today,
With my feet, with my feet.
When I stamp my feet and sing,
I worship God this morning.

I can worship God today,
With my voice, with my voice.
When I shout "amen" and sing,
I worship God this morning.

I can worship God today,
With my arms, with my arms.
When I wave my arms and sing,
I worship God this morning.

**35** Do motions as you sing this prayer song to the tune of *The Mulberry Bush.*

This is the way we fold our hands,
Fold our hands, fold our hands.
This is the way we fold our hands
So we can talk to God.

This is the way we bow our heads,
Bow our heads, bow our heads.
This is the way we bow our heads
So we can talk to God.

**36** This is a great song to lead into a prayer time. Sing it to *Mary Had a Little Lamb.*

Time to talk to Jesus now,
Jesus now, Jesus now.
Time to talk to Jesus now.
Quietly we'll pray.
    Children walk in a circle
Time for us to fold our hands,
Fold our hands, fold our hands.
Time for us to fold our hands.
Quietly we'll pray.
    Children fold hands
Time for us to bow our heads,
Bow our heads, bow our heads.
Time for us to bow our heads.
Quietly we'll pray.
    Children bow heads

**37** Teach this prayer song to the tune of *Twinkle, Twinkle, Little Star.*

We can talk to God each day
    Point up
When we fold our hands to pray.
    Fold hands
Close our eyes and bow our heads
    Do motions mentioned
At the table or in bed.
We can talk to God each day
    Point up
When we fold our hands to pray.
    Fold hands

**38** Children will enjoy marching around the room while singing this song to the tune *Here We Go Looby Loo.*

Here we go to our church,
Here we go to our church,
Here we go to our church,
All on a Sunday morning.

For more verses, substitute these words and actions for the last line of the song:

To hear all the stories of Jesus.
    Point to ears
To pray and sing songs about Jesus.
    Fold hands

**39** Let children make up actions as they sing this next song to the tune of *The Mulberry Bush.*

This is the way we hear God's Word,
Hear God's Word, hear God's Word.
This is the way we hear God's Word
Because we love Him so!

This is the way we give our gifts,
Give our gifts, give our gifts.
This is the way we give our gifts
Because we love Him so!

**40** After singing this song about the Bible, ask children to tell you some reasons why it is special. Use the tune of *London Bridge.*

Listen, listen, to God's Word,
    Put hand up to ear
To God's Word, to God's Word.
Listen, listen, to God's Word;
    Put hand up to other ear
It is special.

**41** Have toddlers hold up a finger for each penny mentioned as they sing these words to the tune of *Ten Little Indians.*

One little, two little, three little pennies
Four little, five little, six little pennies
Seven little, eight little, nine little pennies
Ten little pennies for God.

**42** This fun song has a different action for each verse. Sing to the tune *Ten Little Indians.*

I like singing songs at church. (Repeat 2x)
    Point to mouth
I like songs the best.
I like hearing stories at church. (Repeat 2x)
    Point to ears
I like stories best.
I like making things at church. (Repeat 2x)
    Clap
I like making things.
I like seeing friends at church. (Repeat 2x)
    Point to friends
I like friends the best.
I like everything at church. (Repeat 2x)
    March and clap
I like everything!

**43** This next song is full of fun actions. Sing it to the tune of *Three Blind Mice.*

I thank God. I thank God.
    Point to self
You thank Him, too.
You thank Him, too.
    Point to others
We all come to church and say
"thank You" to God.
    Point up
We meet all our friends and say
"thank You" to God.
    Shake hands
We all bow our heads and say
"thank You" to God.
    Bow heads
Yes, we thank God.
We thank God.
    Fold hands

These next three songs are great for starting class times.

**44** Children may march around the room as they sing these words to the tune *The Mulberry Bush.*

**Now it's time for worship time,**
**Worship time, worship time.**
**Songs and stories, lots of fun,**
**When we come to worship!**

**45** Sing to the tune of *Are You Sleeping?*

**Listen closely, listen closely.**
    Point to ears
**Look and see, look and see.**
    Circle eyes with fingers
**Time to be together,**
**Sharing songs and stories.**
**Come with me. Come with me.**
    Motion to children to follow you

**46** Pass out the rhythm instruments for this song which is sung to the tune of *This Old Man.*

**Worship time, worship time!**
**Come and worship Jesus Christ.**
**We can sing and clap and always we can**
**pray.**
**We can worship every day.**

**47** For this song, divide your class up into groups. Have one group sing the question and the other the answer, then switch groups. Use the tune *Ten Little Indians.*

**What do we do on Sunday morning?**
**What do we do on Sunday morning?**
**What do we do on Sunday morning?**
**We all go to church.**

**48** While singing this song to the tune of *Did You Ever See a Lassie?*, children might enjoy holding hands with a partner and swinging arms along with the rhythm.

**Oh, it's fun to go to my church,**
**To my church, to my church.**
**Oh, it's fun to go to my church.**
**We're God's family.**
**There's Jenny and Michael and Jesse and**
**Carol.**
    Name children as you point to them
**Oh, it's fun to go to my church.**
**We're God's family.**

## Songs About Family and Friends

**49** Teach toddlers this song to the tune of *Skip to My Lou*. Children might enjoy clapping or moving in a circle as they sing.

I love my mommy. Yes, I do!
I love my mommy, Yes, I do.
I love my mommy. Yes, I do!
Thank You, dear God, for Mommy.

For more verses substitute other family names for mommy.

**50** In this song sung to the tune of *Did You Ever See a Lassie?* children can make up their own actions.

We are all a busy family,
A family, a family.
We are all a busy family.
We all help at home.
There's driving, and cooking,
And mowing, and sweeping.
We are all a busy family.
We all help at home.

**51** Have children hold hands and swing arms as they sing this song to the tune of *London Bridge*.

We're a happy family,
Family, family.
God is always helping us
Love each other.

**52** Children will enjoy acting out the next song sung to the tune of *The Farmer in the Dell*.

I have a fam-i-ly.
I have a fam-i-ly.
My family loves and cares for me.
I have a fam-i-ly.
vs. 2 My family cooks my food.
vs. 3 My family buys my clothes.
vs. 4 My family keeps me safe.

**53** Children will be reminded to thank God for their families as they sing this song to the tune of *Twinkle, Twinkle, Little Star*.

Thank You for my family.
    Fold hands as if praying
I'm so glad You gave them to me.
    Big smile, hug arms around self
Brother, sister, Mom and Dad,
    Hold up one finger for each
Each one helps to make me glad.
Thank You for my family
I'm so glad You gave them to me.

**54** Teach children this song to the tune of *Skip to My Lou*.

Shake my hand and be my friend.
    Shake hands
Smile at me and be my friend.
    Smile
We are friends, it's plain to see.
    Join hands in circle
I like you and you like me.
    Drop hands; point to others and self

**55** You can use this song which is sung to the tune *Jesus Loves Me* to remind children to be thankful for their friends. Have them hold hands with a partner and march around the room.

Friends are kind, and friends will share.
They will show their love and care.
Friends are special, yes, indeed.
They will help when you're in need.
Thanks, God, for friends,
Thanks, God, for friends,
Thanks, God, for friends,
A friend will help in need.

Friends are kind, and friends will share.
They will show their love and care.
In my work and in my play,
I will help my friends today.
Thanks, God, for friends,
Thanks, God, for friends,
Thanks, God, for friends,
I'll help my friends today.

**56** Teach children the following words to *London Bridge*.

God wants us to show we care,
Show we care, show we care.
God wants us to show we care.
Here's a great big hug.

Lower the bridge to capture and hug one of the children. Keep your arms around the child and rock back and forth while everyone is singing these words.

Being loving is the way,
Is the way, is the way.
Being loving is the way
To please Jesus.

**57** Here's a friendship song to the tune of *Paw-Paw Patch*.

Who will be my friend this morning?
   (Repeat 2x)
Come and stand beside me.
You're my friend.

During the last line of the song, choose a child to stand beside you and get a handshake or hug of friendship. Repeat that song until all the children who want to have been so honored.

**58** This song will help children learn the names of those in their group. Have toddlers clap as they sing it to *The Farmer in the Dell*.

God gave me special friends. (Repeat)
La-la-la-la-la-la-la-la
God gave me special friends.
My special friend is_____ (insert child's name).
   (Repeat)
La-la-la-la-la-la-la-la
God gave me special friends.

**59** Sing these words to the tune of *Are You Sleeping?*

Who is my friend? Who is my friend?
Maybe you! Maybe you!
You are all my good friends.
You are all my good friends.
You and you. You and you.

Children point to each other on last line

Thank You, God. Thank You, God,
For my friends, For my friends.
You are all my good friends.
You are all my good friends.
You and you. You and you.

**60** Have children sing these words to the tune of **If You're Happy**.

Thank You, God, for giving us our special friends.
   Fold hands
Thank You, God, for giving us our special friends.
   Fold hands
Friends will always show us love.
   Hug self
They're a gift from God above.
   Open arms wide
Thank You, God, for giving us our special friends.
   Fold hands

## Songs About You and Me

**61** Also to the tune of *Are You Sleeping?* is this fun song. Have children sit in a circle. One child is chosen to walk around the circle and gently touch each head as he/she goes around while everyone is singing. When the song ends, the child whose head is last touched is the next to walk around the circle.

We are friends, we are friends,
Yes, we are! Yes, we are!
Sitting in a circle, sitting in a circle.
I like you! I like you!

**62** Have children stand in a circle as they sing this song to *Ten Little Indians.*

One little friend
  Leader chooses a child for the middle
Jesus loves you.
Two little friends
  Leader chooses a second child
Jesus loves you.
Three little friends
  Leader chooses a third child
Jesus loves you.
All join hands and circle 'round.
  Children in the outside circle circle the
  three children on the inside.
Circle 'round all together.
Circle 'round all together.
Circle 'round all together.
It's fun to play as friends.

**63** Sing these words to the tune of *There's a Hole in the Bucket.* On the last line, do the action indicated.

I'll thank God for making my hands,
my hands.
I'll clap with my hands
La-la-la-la-la.
I'll thank God for making my feet,
my feet.
I'll march with my feet
La-la-la-Ia-la.
I'll thank God for making my voice,
my voice.
I'll sing with my voice
La-la-la-la-la.

**64** Do motions and sing these words to the tune of *Jesus Loves the Little Children.*

Grown-ups love the little children,
All the children everywhere.
When they sing and when they pray,
When they eat and when they play,
Grown-ups love the little children every-
where.

**65** Children will love this next action rhyme sung to the tune of *Row, Row, Row Your Boat.*

God made hands and hair,
  Hold up hands, then touch hair
Eyes and nose and knees.
  Point to body parts mentioned
Thank You, thank You, thank You, God,
  Turn in a circle
For making all of me!
  Point to self

**66** Sing these words to the tune of *Jingle Bells*, pointing to the body part mentioned.

Head and toes,
Arms and nose,
Shoulders, ears, and knees.
Thank You, God, for making every
Little part of me!

**67** Have children move the body parts mentioned in each verse of this action rhyme. Sing to the tune of *The Mulberry Bush*.

Thank You, God, for my two hands
My two hands, my two hands.
Thank You, God, for my two hands
I use my hands to praise you.

For other verses substitute "feet" or "all of me" for "hands."

**68** Children will enjoy clapping their hands as they sing this song to the tune of *The Farmer in the Dell*.

Jesus was like me.
Jesus was like me.
Jesus had a family.
Jesus was like me.

For more verses, substitute these words for the third line of the song:

vs. 2 Jesus grew up wise and tall.
vs. 3 Jesus liked to talk of God.
vs. 4 Jesus liked to help His friends.

**69** This song which is sung to *Are You Sleeping?* can be a group song with children seated in a circle.

(Leader or parent)
Where is _____ (insert child's name)?
Where is _____ ?
Here I am! Here I am!
(Leader or parent)
Jesus loves you, Jesus loves you
Yes, He does!
Yes, He does!

**70** Sing these words to the tune of *Twinkle, Twinkle, Little Star*.

When I'm running at the park
Run, in place
When I'm sleeping and it's dark
Rest cheek on hands
When I swim out in the sun
Pretend to swim
When I look at books for fun
Open hands, palms up
In everything I do or say,
Stretch arms wide
God is with me every day.
Hug self

**71** Children will have lots of fun with this action song sung to *If You're Happy*.

I am growing and I know it; I can clap.
I am growing and I know it; I can clap.
I am growing and I know it.
I am growing and I know it.
I am growing and I know it; I can clap.

For more verses, substitute "march," "jump," and "shout" for "clap" and do the actions.

## Songs About Helping

**72** Have toddlers join hands and swing arms together as they sing these words to the tune of *Mary Had a Little Lamb.*

Let's be kind to everyone
Everyone, everyone.
Let's be kind to everyone
As Jesus said to do.
Let's love God and others, too
Others, too, others, too.
Let's love God and others, too
As Jesus said to do.

Let's be kind and let's forgive
Let's forgive, let's forgive.
Let's be kind and let's forgive,
As Jesus said to do.

**73** Sing these words to the tune of *Praise Him, Praise Him* as children clap their hands in rhythm.

Listen, listen, all you little children
Love the Lord, love the Lord.
Listen, listen, all you little children
Love the Lord, love the Lord.

For more verses, substitute these lines for the first and third:

Obey Him, obey Him, all you little children

Thank Him, thank Him, all you little children

Give gifts, give gifts, all you little children

Help work, help work, all you little children

**74** Sign language can be used for each gift mentioned in this song sung to *Skip to My Lou.*

Love, love, love In my heart,
Love, love, love In my heart,
Love, love, love in my heart,
Love is a gift from Jesus.
vs. 2 Peace
vs. 3 Joy

**75** Have children make up their own actions for this song sung to the tune of *London Bridge.*

I can help to fold the clothes,
Fold the clothes, fold the clothes.
I show God I like to help
When I fold the clothes.
vs. 2 I can help to wash the spoons
vs. 3 I can help to dust the chairs

**76** Children will enjoy singing these songs as they help with cleaning the room. Sing to *Are You Sleeping?*

I'm a helper. I'm a helper.
   Point to self on the word "I"
Yes, I am! Yes, I am!
I can help my _____. (insert mommy, daddy, teacher, etc.)
I can help my _____. (insert name)
Pick up toys! Pick up toys!

**77** Sing these words to the tune of *This Old Man* as children are helping with cleanup.

Pick up toys. Pick up toys.
Cleanup time for girls and boys.
Soon our room will look so nice and clean and neat.
Use your helping hands and feet.

**78** Clap hands and sing these words to the tune of *Are You Sleeping?*

Time to clean up. Time to clean up.
Yes, it is. Yes, it is.
You are all good helpers.
You are all good helpers.
Yes, you are. Yes, you are.

**79** Sing these words to the tune of *The Mulberry Bush* while toddlers move around in a circle.

Jesus loves all boys and girls,
Boys and girls, boys and girls.
Jesus loves all boys and girls,
He is God's special Son.

Jesus came for all of us,
All of us, all of us.
Jesus came for all of us,
He is God's special Son.
Jesus lives for you and me,
You and me, you and me.
Jesus lives for you and me,
He is God's special Son.

Jesus hears us when we pray,
When we pray, when we pray.
Jesus hears us when we pray,
He is God's special Son.

Jesus is with us today,
Us today, us today.
Jesus is with us today,
He is God's special Son.

**80** Play rhythm instruments as you sing this happy Easter song to the tune *Jingle Bells*.

Easter's here. Let us cheer.
Jesus is alive.
Say, "Hooray!" It's Easter Day.
Jesus is alive.

**81** Children will enjoy this next Easter song which is sung to the tune of *There's a Hole in the Bucket.*

There's a joy in my heart now;
  Make a happy face
It's Easter. It's Easter.
  Clap twice
There's a joy in my heart now;
It's Easter today!
There is love in my heart now;
  Hug self
It's Easter. It's Easter.
  Clap twice
There is love in my heart now;
It's Easter today!
There is peace in my heart now;
  Place hand over heart
It's Easter. It's Easter.
  Clap twice
There is peace in my heart now;
It's Easter today!
There's a song in my heart now;
  Clap hands throughout the verse
It's Easter. It's Easter.
There's a song in my heart now;
It's Easter today!

**82** Sing these words to the tune of *Here We Go Looby Lou.* Do the actions indicated.

Let's clap our hands and shout.
Let's sing a song of praise.
Let's clap our hands and shout.
Jesus is with us today!

**83** Here's a Mother's Day song to the tune of *This Old Man.*

I love Mom.
  Point to self then out
Mom loves me.
  Point out then to self
I am happy as can be.
  Make happy face
Mom, you're nice,
As nice as any mom can be.
I'm glad God gave you to me!
  Clap hands on last two lines

Other family members' names can be substituted for the word "mom."

**84** Here's a great Mother's or Father's Day song you can teach your toddlers to sing to their parents at home. It is sung to the tune of *London Bridge.*

Dad, I love you. Yes, I do!
Yes, I do! Yes, I do!
  Shake head "yes" each time word is mentioned
Dad, I love you. Yes, I do!
Happy Father's Day!

**85** Have children sit down quickly on the last line of this song sung to the tune *Ring Around the Rosey.*

Thank You, God, for food.
Thank You, God, for food.
Thank You, thank You,
We all thank You.

**86** These words maybe taught to the tune of *Down by the Station.* Clap as you sing.

Let's sing a song now
All about Thanksgiving.
Let's sing a song now.
Sing it to the Lord.
Thank Him for our families.
Thank Him for the good food.
Let's sing a song now.
Sing It to the Lord.

**87** Toddlers will express their thanks to God for things He's given them as they sing this next song to the tune of *If You're Happy*. Follow the motions.

If you're thankful for your food,
raise your hand.
If you're thankful for your food,
raise your hand.
If you're thankful for your food,
If you're thankful for your food,
If you're thankful for your food,
raise your hand.

For more verses, use "clothes," "toys," or "family" for the word "food."

**88** Sing this happy Christmas song to the tune of *Twinkle, Twinkle, Little Star*.

Listen, listen carefully.
> Cup hands by ears

Come and share good news with me!
> Beckon towards yourself

Here's the news for everyone.
> Cup hands by ears

God sent us His only Son.
> Point to heaven

In a little manger stall.
> Fold arms as if rocking a baby

Jesus came for one and all.

For the last two lines of the song substitute these lines to make more verses:

vs. 2 **Shepherds sleeping in the night.**
> Fold hands by head as if sleeping

**Heard good news by angels' light.**

vs. 3 **Wise men worshiped Him its true.**
> Fold hands and bow head.

**We can worship Jesus, too.**
> Point to self

**89** Lead toddlers in singing this Christmas song to the tune of *She'll Be Comin' Round the Mountain When She Comes*. Act out each verse.

Jesus was a little baby in the hay.
Jesus was a little baby in the hay.
Jesus was a little baby,
Jesus was a little baby,
Jesus was a little baby in the hay.

There were cattle in the barn by Jesus' bed.
There were cattle in the barn by Jesus' bed.
There were cattle in the barn,
There were cattle in the barn,
There were cattle in the barn by Jesus' bed.

vs. 3 **Shepherds came in very softly with the sheep …**

vs. 4 **Wise men praised the baby Jesus as a king …**

**90** For this song sung to *Jingle Bells*, give children their own bells to ring. You might want to attach small jingle bells to a tinsel pipe cleaner and twist to make a bracelet for each child.

Christmastime!
Christmastime!
Christmastime is here!
We are glad that Jesus came.
Let's clap our hands and cheer!

**91** Toddlers can review the whole Christmas story by marching around the room and singing this song to *London Bridge*.

Mary heard the happy news,
Happy news, happy news.
Mary heard the happy news:
God sent Jesus.
Jesus born In Bethlehem,
Bethlehem, Bethlehem.
Jesus born In Bethlehem.
God sent Jesus.

Angels gave the shepherds news,
Shepherds news, shepherds news.
Angels gave the shepherds news,
God sent Jesus.

Wise men came to worship Him,
Worship Him, worship Him.
Wise men came to worship Him.
God sent Jesus.

We can share the good news, too,
Good news, too, good news, too.
We can share the good news, too.
God sent Jesus.

**92** Let children march around the room as they sing this next song to *Skip to My Lou*. On the last line of each verse, have them stop and point up to heaven.

Have you heard the happy news?
Have you heard the happy news?
Have you heard the happy news?
God sent His Son, Jesus.

Late at night the angels sang.
Late at night the angels sang.
Late at night the angels sang.
God sent His Son, Jesus.

Shepherds ran to Bethlehem.
Shepherds ran to Bethlehem.
Shepherds ran to Bethlehem.
God sent His Son, Jesus.

**93** Teach these words to the tune of *Twinkle, Twinkle, Little Star*. Have children do the actions.

Clap your hands now, 1-2-3.
Touch your ears,
And touch your knees.
Wiggle fingers.
Wiggle toes.
Shake your head and
Hold your nose.
God made every part of me.
I can sit down quietly.

**94** Teach toddlers about praising the Lord through this next song sung to *The Farmer in the Dell*.

I can praise the Lord.
I can praise the Lord.
I can praise God with a clap.
I can praise the Lord.

Children may suggest words to replace "clap" to tell other ways to praise God such as "jump," "smile," or "shout."

**95** Praise the Lord together with your toddlers as you march around and sing this song to the tune *London Bridge*.

March along and sing a song
Sing a song, sing a song.
March along and sing a song
Happy morning!
vs. 2 March along and clap your hands ...
vs. 3 March along and stamp your feet ...
vs. 4 March along and shout "amen" ...

**96** See if toddlers can follow you as you sing and act out this song to the tune of *This Old Man*.

Flap your arms.
Touch your shoe.
Clap your hands now 1 and 2!
You can stamp your feet,
And make a funny face!
Then you sit down
In your place.

**97** Teach this action song to the tune of *Row, Row, Row Your Boat*. Have children start in a crouching position then "grow" as they sing.

Up, up, up we go
Till we're very tall.
*(Continued on next page.)*
Slowly, slowly we go down.
Now we're very small.

Up, up, up we go.
Give your hands a clap.
Turn around and then sit down.
Your hands fold in your lap.

**98** Here's another action song sung to the tune of *Twinkle, Twinkle, Little Star*.

Stand right up and stretch so tall.
Now sit down. We'll all be small.
Twist and twist and twist around.
Reach way down and touch the ground.
Touch your ear and touch your knee.
Now we sit down quietly.

**99** Have children follow you and sing these words to the tune of *Ring Around the Rosey*.

Come and follow me.
Come and follow me.
Follow, follow
All around the room.
Come and clap with me.
Come and clap with me.
Clapping, clapping
All around the room.

**100** Children will enjoy doing this movement song to *She'll Be Comin' Round the Mountain*.

Can you clap your hands together just like me?
Can you clap your hands together just like me?
Can you clap your hands together?
Can you clap your hands together?
Can you clap your hands together just like me?

Other verses might include:
Can you march around the circle?
Can you bend your knees and straighten?
Can you make your body wiggle?

# 100 Action Songs for Ages 3-5

## Songs About Jesus and God

**1** This action rhyme is sung to the tune of *The Farmer in the Dell.* Teach the words and actions to your pupils.

**God sends the rain to fall.**
> Raise, then lower arms, wiggling fingers

**God sends the shining sun.**
> Touch fingertips overhead

**And Jesus lives to show the world**
> Raise arms high

**God's love for everyone.**
> Hug self

**2** Sing the following song to the tune of *Mulberry Bush.* Children may clap as they sing, use the actions, or join hands and walk in a circle.

**Jesus is a Friend of mine,**
> Point up, then to self

**Friend of mine, Friend of mine.**
> Point to self

**Jesus is a Friend of mine,**
**He'll always be with me.**
> Nod and hug self

Alternate last lines:

**I'll thank him every day.**
> Point to self; fold hands in prayer

**He listens when I pray.**
> Point up, then to ears; fold hands

**The Bible tells me so.**
> Hold hands together to make a book

**3** Teach children this action rhyme to *The Farmer in the Dell.*

**The flowers bloom so bright.**
> Wrists together, palms open

**The birds fly high and free.**
> Arms high, wave hands

**I know God cares for all these things.**
> Spread arms wide

**I feel His love for me.**
> Hug self

**4** Sing the following words to the tune *London Bridge Is Falling Down.* Children can clap as they sing or join hands and walk in circle.

**Jesus wants me to be good,**
**To be good,**
**To be good.**
**Jesus wants me to be good.**
**He will help me.**

**Jesus wants me to forgive,**
**To forgive,**
**To forgive,**
**Jesus wants me to forgive.**
**He will help me.**

**5** Teach children these words and actions to the song *Jesus Loves Me.* Use these words for the verse, but sing the traditional words for the chorus.

**Jesus always hears me pray.**
> Fold hands

**Jesus watches over me.**
> Shade eyes with hands

**Jesus loves me everyday**
> Hug self

**And He helps my family.**
> Point up, then make roof with hands

**6** Sing this verse to the tune *Farmer in the Dell.* It can be sung as a prayer.

**Dear Lord, I love You.**
**Dear Lord, I love You.**
**Because You love me as You do,**
**Yes, Lord, I love You.**

**7** This fun action rhyme is sung to *London Bridge*. You might want to rehearse the words with the tune ahead of time. One syllable goes with each note of the melody.

**I'm so glad that God made me!**
Point to self
**And all things that I see.**
Arms wide
**Plants that start as seeds so small.**
Squat low
**Growing, growing tall.**
Stand up slowly and reach high
**Elephants with trunks so long.**
Join hands in front to form trunk
**Birds that sing a sweet song.**
Flap arms as if flying
**Fishes swimming to and fro,**
Palms together, move hands zigzag
**Dogs that bark to say "hello!"**
Bark like puppy dogs

**8** Have children join hands and stand in a circle. Have them sing these words to *Mulberry Bush*.

**Jesus said, "Obey God's Word,**
**Obey God's Word, obey God's Word."**
**Jesus said, "Obey God's Word."**
**Obey God's Word today.**

Have children walk in a circle. Stop after you sing the song, and ask two or three children to name one way they can obey God's Word. (Praying, helping, being kind, etc.) Then sing the song again, asking other children how they can obey. Continue until each child has a chance to respond.

**9** This action rhyme can be sung to the tune *Three Blind Mice*.

**God made you.**
Point to a friend
**God made me.**
Point to self
**God made you.**
**God made me.**
**God made all of my family**
Spread arms out

**God made animals, plants, and trees.**
Clap in rhythm
**God made everyone I can see.**
Look around room, shading eyes with hands
**A great God is He.**
Raise arms in praise

**10** Have children clap as they sing these words to *The Farmer in the Dell*.

**I'm H-A-P-P-Y,**
**I'm H-A-P-P-Y,**
**I know that Jesus is alive,**
**I'm H-A-P-P-Y.**

**11** Sing these words to the tune *Did You Ever See a Lassie?*

**I am glad we have the Bible,**
**The Bible, the Bible.**
**I am glad we have the Bible**
**To learn of our Friend.**
**Our Friend's name is Jesus.**
**Our Friend's name is Jesus.**
**I am glad we have the Bible**
**To learn of our Friend.**

**12** Teach your children the words and actions to this song. Sing it to the tune of *Twinkle, Twinkle, Little Star*.

**Who made trees that reach so high?**
Stretch arms high; bend in wind
**God made trees and birds that fly**
Stretch arms high; flap arms
**Who made flowers that bend in the breeze?**
Head and shoulders sway in circular motion
**God made flowers and all the bees.**
Sway as above; hold hands up by shoulders, flutter hands rapidly
**Who made grass as green as can be?**
Stoop and move hands as if feeling grass
**God made grass and God made ME!**
Feel grass; stand up and point to self

**13** Lead pupils in a variation of *The Farmer in the Dell.*

Pick a carpenter to stand in the circle and pretend to pound.

**The carpenter fixes the roof.**
**The carpenter fixes the roof.**
**This is work he does for God.**
**He loves to fix the roof.**

Pick a janitor to stand in the circle and pretend to sweep.

**The janitor sweeps the floor.**
**The janitor sweeps the floor.**
**This is work he does for God.**
**He loves to sweep the floor.**

Pick a teacher to stand in the circle and pretend to hold a book.

**The teacher teaches the class.**
or use teacher's name
**The teacher teaches the class.**
**This is work she/he does for God.**
**She/He loves to teach the class.**

Pick a pastor to stand in the circle and pretend to hold a Bible.

**The pastor tells about God.**
**The pastor tells about God.**
**This is work he does for God.**
**The pastor tells about God.**

Everyone join hands and sing.
**All of us love God.**
**All of us love God.**
**We have work that we can do.**
**All of us love God.**

**14** Sing the following words to *Happy Birthday.* You will sing the first part as a question, and the children will answer, "I do." You may need to help them answer the first time you sing this. Point to them when it is their turn to sing.

**Who loves Jesus? (I do.)**
**Who loves Jesus? (I do.)**
**Who loves Jesus? Who loves Jesus?**
**Who loves Jesus? (I do.)**

**15** Sing these action words to The *Farmer in the Dell.*

**When I'm at rest or play**
Lean head on folded hands, then run in place
**God watches over me.**
Point up, then shield eyes with hands
**For everything God gives each day,**
Spread arms wide, then point up
**I'll thank Him joyfully.**
Extend arms forward and up in praise

**16** These words and actions are sung to *Mary Had a Little Lamb.* Each verse will have different actions. For the first verse, pick a child to be in the middle of a circle. The child pantomimes a flower growing by stooping down and rising slowly while other children walk around him or her singing:

**I'm a flower growing tall,**
**Growing tall, growing tall.**
**I'm a flower growing tall.**
**God takes care of me.**

Now children stop walking, and all pantomime the sunshine by raising their arms in a circle above their heads.

**God will send the sunshine bright,**
**Sunshine bright, sunshine bright.**
**God will send the sunshine bright.**
**God takes care of me.**

Pick another child to stand in the middle and pantomime a bird by flapping his or her arms up and down. Other children walk in a circle.

**I'm a bird that flies so high,**
**Flies so high, flies so high.**
**I'm a bird that flies so high.**
**God takes care of me.**

Now pupils stop walking and cup their hands to form a nest.

**God gives twigs to build a nest,**
**Build a nest, build a nest.**
**God gives twigs to build a nest.**
**God takes care of me.**

**17** This action rhyme may be sung to *London Bridge.*

**Who does Jesus help and love?**
  Hold hands out, palms up
**Look and see! Look and see!**
  Circle eyes with fingers
**Who does Jesus help and love?**
  Hold hands out palms up
**You and you and me!**
  Point to children, then self

**18** Sing the following words to the tune of *Twinkle, Twinkle Little Star.*

**I love Jesus. Does He know?**
**Do I ever tell Him so?**
**I can tell Him every day.**
**Showing love in lots of ways.**
**I love Jesus. Yes, He knows.**
**And I love to tell him so.**

**19** Teach children the following words to the tune *Mary Had a Little Lamb.*

**Lord, I love You-yes, I do!**
**Yes, I do! Yes I do!**
**Lord, I love You-yes, I do,**
**Because You love me so.**

After singing the song a couple of times select a child to name in the song.

**Todd loves Jesus-yes, he does!**
**Yes, he does! Yes, he does!**
**Todd loves Jesus-yes, he does,**
**Because He loves him so.**

Conclude by singing:

**He is with me all the time,**
**All the time, all the time.**
**He is with me all the time.**
**Jesus is my Friend.**

**20** Sing this action rhyme to *Twinkle, Twinkle, Little Star.*

**God made trees that grow so tall,**
  Raise arms and stand on tiptoes
**And the little ants so small.**
  Squat down
**Apples red, the big bright sun,**
  Make small circle with hands, then large circle with arms
**Stars that shine when day is done.**
  Wiggle finger to show twinkling stars
**Mommies, daddies, babies, too.**
  Pretend to rock baby
**God made me, and God made you.**
  Point to self then someone else

**21** Play a variation of the game, *London Bridge,* with your pupils. Have two pupils form a bridge by joining hands and holding their arms up while the other pupils line up and walk under the bridge. Have children sing these words as they play:

**God is with me all the time,**
**All the time, all the time.**
**God is with me all the time,**
**He is with me.**

On the last line the bridge should come down gently around one child. That child should name a place where God is with him or her. For example, **God is with me at the store.**

**22** Let pairs of children march around the room, singing the following words to *Mulberry Bush.*

**I'm so glad that God loves me.**
**God loves me. God loves me.**
**I'm so glad that God loves me.**
**He gave me a friend.**

**23** Help children join hands and form a circle. Have them walk in a circle as they sing these words to *The Farmer in the Dell.*

**God takes care of me.**
**God takes care of me.**
**God takes care of everything,**
**And God takes care of me.**

Have children stop walking, stand in place, and crouch down, pretending they are little seeds. Explain to them that God sends sunlight and rain to help seeds grow. Slowly the children begin to stretch, getting bigger and bigger. Have children circle their heads with their arms. Now they pretend to be beautiful flowers. Sing the song again using the words "little seeds" in place of "everything." Continue the game, varying the pantomime. Other ideas are trees blowing, birds flying, rabbits hopping, fish swimming.

**24** Sing this action rhyme to the tune of *Twinkle, Twinkle, Little Star.*

**God made the land, and God made the sea.**
  Hold hands out, palms down
**God made it all, and God loves me.**
  Arms wide, then point to self
**God made day and the sun so bright.**
  Touch fingertips overhead
**God made the moon and stars at night.**
  Wiggle fingers for stars twinkling
**God made the land, and God made the sea.**
  Hold hands out, palms down
**God made it all, and God loves me.**
  Arms wide, then point to self

**25** This fun action song is sung to *If You're Happy and You Know It.*

**From my head down to my toes,**
  Touch head, then toes
**God made me.**
  Spread arms wide, then bring them together and clap twice
**From my head down to my toes,**
**God made me.**

**From my head down to my toes,**
  Touch head, then toes
**And my eyes and ears and nose,**
  Point to eyes, ears, and nose
**From my head down to my toes,**
**God made me.**

**26** Play a variation of *London Bridge.* Pick two children to form a bridge. As the other children walk under the bridge, sing these words:

**Jesus loves us; yes, He does,**
**Yes He does; yes, He does.**
**Jesus loves us; yes, He does,**
**He loves (name of child "caught").**
As the bridge gently sways back and forth with the "caught" child, sing these words to the chorus of Jesus Loves Me.

**Yes, Jesus loves you.**
**Yes, Jesus loves you.**
**Yes, Jesus loves you.**
**He loves everyone!**

The "caught" child then exchanges places with one of the children forming the bridge.

**27** Have children join hands and walk in a circle as they sing these words to the tune *Mulberry Bush.*

**God goes with me everywhere,**
**Everywhere, everywhere.**
**God goes with me everywhere,**
**Everywhere I go.**
**Jesus is a Friend of mine.**
**I can trust Him all the time.**
**When I'm home or far away,**
**He is with me every day.**

Ask children to name places where God is with them. Use that suggestion in the song and do an appropriate motion as you continue to walk in a circle. Allow each child to name a place.

**28** Have children stand in a circle and do actions with you as they sing these words to *Mulberry Bush*.

**I thank God for my strong legs,**
  Shake one leg
**My strong legs, my strong legs.**
**I thank God for my strong legs.**
  Shake the other leg
**See how high I jump.**
  Jump in place
**I thank God for my strong hands,**
  Clap hands
**My strong hands, my strong hands.**
**I thank God for my strong hands.**
  Continue to clap
**See how fast I clap.**
  Clap hands faster
**I thank God for my fast feet,**
  Run in place
**My fast feet, my fast feet.**
**I thank God for my fast feet.**
  Continue to run in place slowly
**See how fast I run.**
  Run in place faster

**29** Sing these words and actions to the tune *Ten Little Indians*.

**Thank You for the hat on my head.**
  Place hands on head
**Thank You for my apple, round and red.**
  Touch fingertips to form a circle
**Thank You for my family**
  Touch fingertips overhead to form roof
**Thank You, God, for me.**
  Hug self

**30** Sing these words to the tune The *Farmer in the Dell*.

**The flowers on the hill,**
  Pretend to pick a flower and smell it
**The birds up in the tree,**
  Flap arms to imitate a bird flying
**God takes care of all of them,**
  Spread arms in wide gesture
**And God takes care of me!**
  Point to chest with both index fingers

**31** Children stand in various places throughout the room and sing these words to the tune *Are You Sleeping?*

Teacher:
**Where is (Cindy)?**
**Where is (Cindy)?**
Pupil:
**Here I am!**
**Here I am!**
Teacher:
**Is Jesus with you?**
**Is Jesus with you?**
Pupil:
**Yes, He is!**
**Yes, He is;**
Teacher:
**Where is Jesus?**
**Where is Jesus?**
Pupils:
**He is here!**
**He is here!**
Teacher:
**Jesus never leaves us.**
**He is always with us.**
Pupils:
**Thank You, Lord!**
**Thank You, Lord!**

**32** Seat children in a circle, and teach them these words to *London Bridge*.

**Jesus loves us, big and small,**
**Big and small, big and small.**
**Jesus loves us, big and small,**
**JESUS LOVES US!**

Have children stand up on the word "big" and sit down on the word "small". On the last line, have them sing louder and clap the rhythm.

**33** Sing this Bible story action rhyme to the tune *Are You Sleeping?*

**Fishermen,**
> Gesture people to come

**Fishermen, Pick up your nets.**
> Pretend to pick up heavy net

**Pick up your nets. Throw them in the sea.**
> Pretend to toss it out to sea

**Pull in all the fish.**
> Pretend to pull the net back in

**Come, follow Me!**
> Motion to come

**Come, follow Me!**

**34** Sing these words and actions to the tune *Mulberry Bush.*

**Head and shoulders and knees and toes,**
> Touch each part with hands

**Head and shoulders and knees and toes,**
**Head and shoulders and knees and toes,**
**God made all of me.**
> Spread arms wide

Alternate last line: **I am growing up!**

Other words:

**Arms and legs and feet and hands ...**
**Ears and eyes and mouth and tongue ...**

**35** Teach your pupils these words to *The Farmer in the Dell.*

**I'm glad that God made day.**
**I'm glad that God made day.**
**That's the time I run and play.**
**I'm glad that God made day.**
**I'm glad that God made night.**
**I'm glad that God made night.**
**That's the time my eyes shut tight.**
**I'm glad that God made night.**
**I'm glad God made the sun.**
**I'm glad God made the sun.**
**God loves us very, very much.**
**I'm glad God made the sun.**

Allow each child to select one object of Creation that the class can sing about.

**36** This action song helps young children learn how Jesus wants them to act. Sing these words to *London Bridge.*

**Jesus wants me to be kind,**
> Raise arms, palms up

**To be kind, to be kind.**
> Join hands with classmates

**Jesus wants me to be kind.**
> Raise joined hands

**Kindness makes me happy!**
> Clap to rhythm of words

**Jesus helps me give and share,**
> Raise arms, palms up

**Give and share, give and share.**
> Pretend to hand something to someone

**Jesus helps me give and share.**
**Sharing makes me happy.**
**Jesus wants me to do my work**
**Do my work, do my work**
> Pantomime a job like sweeping

**Jesus wants me to do my work.**
**I will do it!**
> Point to self, nod, and smile

**Jesus gives me rules to live,**
**Rules to live, rules to live.**
> Form hands like open Bible

**Jesus gives me rules to live.**
**I'll obey Him!**
> Clap to rhythm

**Jesus loves me all the time,**
> Hug self

**All the time, all the time.**
> March in place

**He forgives me when I'm wrong,**
> Fold hands in prayer

**He still loves me.**
> Hug self

**37** Have pupils join hands and walk in a circle as they sing these words to *Do You Know the Muffin Man?*

Do you know who made the seas,
Who made the seas,
Who made the seas?
Do you know who made the seas,
Who made the seas for us?
The Bible says God made the seas,
God made the seas,
God made the seas.
The Bible says God made the seas.
He made the seas for us.

Use any object of Creation in place of "seas".

**38** Teach children this Bible story action rhyme to *Happy Birthday.*

One boy had two fish
    Hold up one finger, then two
And five loaves of bread.
    Hold up five fingers
He shared them with Jesus
    Hold hands out, palms up
Lots of people were fed.
    Wiggle fingers to indicate many people

**39** These words can be sung to *Mulberry Bush* as children march around the room.

This is the way we go to church,
Go to church, go to church.
This is the way we go to church,
So early in the morning.
Here we are in Sunday School,
Sunday School, Sunday SchooL
Here we are in Sunday School,
So early In the morning.
Look who came to Sunday School,
To Sunday School, to Sunday School.
Look who came to Sunday School.
Look who came today.

Sing each pupil's first name in place of the words "look who". Continue until each child's name has been sung.

Here are additional verses that can be sung with actions.

This is the way we dress for church.
    Pretend to put on clothing
This is the way we pray at church.
    Fold hands as in prayer
This is the way we sing at church.
    Pretend to use a hymnal

**40** Sing these words to *Mary Had a Little Lamb.* Then substitute each child's name for "you".

I'm so glad you came today,
Came today, came today.
I'm so glad you came today,
Came to Sunday School.

**41** This action song is sung to *The Farmer in the Dell.*

**I use my feet to walk.**
> Point to feet; walk in place

**I use my mouth to pray.**
> Point to mouth

**I use my ears to hear God's Word.**
> Point to ears

**I worship him this way.**
> Nod head

**42** Teach the children these words and actions to the tune *The Farmer in the Dell.*

**God is a special Friend.**
> Point up, then to self

**He listens when we pray.**
> Cup hand behind ear, then fold hands

**He wants us all to come to church,**
> Walk in place or around room

**On this His special day.**
> Spread arms up and wide in praise

**43** Place a piece of tape on the floor. Have children join hands and walk in a circle as they sing these words to *London Bridge.*

**Oh, we love to go to church,**
**Go to church, go to church.**
**Oh, we love to go to church.**
**Can you tell me why?**

The child who lands nearest the piece of tape should tell one thing he or she likes about Sunday School. You could vary this activity by singing these words:

**What does our money help to buy**
**Help to buy help to buy?**
**What does our money help to buy?**
**It buys...**

**44** These words may be sung while children walk in a circle. They may be sung to either *Mary Had a Little Lamb* or *Mulberry Bush.*

**Sunday is a happy day,**
**Happy day, happy day.**
**Sunday is a happy day.**
**We will sing together.**
**Now it's time for us to sing,**
**For us to sing, for us to sing.**
**Now it's time for us to sing**
**On this happy morning.**

**45** Teach pupils these words to *Row, Row, Row Your Boat.* Let children play follow the leader throughout the classroom. Change leaders and actions after each singing. Children might tiptoe, hop one one foot, skip, walk while patting their heads, etc.

**Come, oh, come with me.**
**Learn to sing and pray.**
**Come with me to Sunday School.**
**Have a happy day.**

**46** Teach your pupils the following words and motions to *The Farmer in the Dell.*

**I can talk to God,**
> Point to self, to mouth, and up

**I can talk to God,**
**God listens when I pray to Him,**
> Point up, to ear, to self; then fold hands in prayer

**That's when I talk to God.**

## Songs About Family

**47** In a prominent place, have Bibles, Sunday School books, teaching aid pictures, and crayons. Teach your pupils the following song to the tune *Ten Little Indians*.

One little, two little, three little pennies,
Four little, five little, six little pennies,
Seven little, eight little, nine little pennies,
Ten pennies help to buy...
Repeat tune right away.
Bibles and books, pictures and crayons,
Bibles and books, pictures and crayons,
Bibles and books, pictures and crayons,
To use in Sunday School.

**48** Teach pupils these words and actions to *Twinkle, Twinkle, Little Star*.

I look in the Bible to see
    Hold open hands together
Just what God is saying to me.
    Point to self
Worship God and always obey.
    Raise arms over head
Talk to Jesus every day.
    Fold hands and bow head
I look in the Bible to see
Just what God is saying to me.

**49** Sing to the tune of *London Bridge Is Falling Down*.

I can learn to help at home,
    Point to self; form a roof with hands.
Help at home, help at home.
I can learn to help at home.
Jesus helps me.
    Point up; point to self.
I can learn to share my toys,
    Point to self; hold out hands.
Share my toys, share my toys.
I can learn to share my toys.
Jesus helps me.
    Point up; point to self.

**50** Line up children in single file. Join hands with an assistant or older child and raise your arms to form a bridge. Have an assistant walk the line of children under your arms, around you, and under your arms again while you sing the following words to *London Bridge Is Falling Down*.

What do your parents say to do,
Say to do, say to do?
What do your parents say to do?
Do you obey?

Bring your arms down gently on the last line of the song, and "capture" the child going under them. That pupil must tell you one thing his parents tell him to do at home, such as pick up toys, go to bed, eat all his supper, etc. Ask the child if he obeys. When he says "Yes," he may replace your assistant or other pupil and join hands with you to become part of the bridge. Continue until each child has had a turn. If your class is large, you might want to capture two pupils at a time so the game won't go on too long.

A variation of this action song uses the following words:

What do your parents do for you?
Do for you, do for you?
What do your parents do for you?
Will you tell us?        *(Continued on next page.)*

When the bridge comes down during the last line, the child may tell one thing that a parent does for him or her.

**51** These words help children think of ways they can show love to their families. It is sung to the tune of *Mulberry Bush*.

**This is the way we show our love,**
**Show our love, show our love,**
**This is the way we show our love**
**Every single day.**

Have children share ways they can express affection, like giving hugs, saying "I love you," etc. Then help children to understand that another way they can show their families they love them is by helping. Have pupils act out such things as picking up toys, sweeping, emptying trash.

**52** These words help remind children of things they can do to take care of themselves. The melody is *Mulberry Bush*. Children should act out the words they are singing.

**This is the way we wash our face,**
**Wash our face, wash our face.**
**This is the way we wash our face,**
**So early in the morning.**

Other verses:

**This is the way we wash our hands.**
**This is the way we comb our hair.**
**This is the way we eat our food.**
**This is the way we exercise.**
**This is the way we go to sleep.**
**This is the way we read our books.**

**53** This song may be sung to the tune of *The Farmer in the Dell*. Children may praise God by clapping as they sing or march around the room.

**God made my family,**
**God made my family,**
**He gives me everything I need,**
**God made my family,**

Other ways this can be sung are God made my mom and dad, etc. Encourage children to sing the following words at home to their families:

**Oh, I love you today,**
**Oh, I love you today.**
**I'm so glad that you're my friend.**
**I love you today.**

**54** These words may be sung to *Twinkle, Twinkle, Little Star*.

**God gave me a family**
   Point up; hug self
**And a home where I can be**
   Form roof over head with hands
**Happy, safe, and free to do**
   Point to mouth and smile
**Lots of things, exciting and new.**
   Spread arms wide; jump up and down
**We all work together and play**
   Pretend to sweep floor; then throw ball
**And eat the food God gives each day.**
   Pretend to eat; point up

**55** Have children join hands and walk in a circle. Have them walk in the opposite direction for the second verse. Sing words to the tune of *Mulberry Bush*.

**I thank God for my family**
**my family, my family.**
**I thank God for my family,**
**My mother and my dad.**
**I thank God for my family,**
**My family, my family**
**I thank God for my family**
**My sister and my brother.**

## Songs About Children and Helping

**56** Sing this song about ways children can help at home to the tune *The Farmer in the Dell.*

**When Mom and Dad clean house,**
　Sweep with a broom
**There's work for me to do.**
　Point to self
**I help them shake out all the rugs,**
　Shake rugs vigorously
**And empty baskets, too.**
　Lift, carry, and empty baskets
**I help them dig our garden.**
　Pretend to dig with shovel
**I give my dog a drink.**
　Pour water into dog's dish
**For we are all a family**
　Extend arms as if to hug family
**It's fun to help, I think!**
　Draw smile on face with fingertip.

**57** Sing these words for special days to the tune of *Happy Birthday.*

**Happy Father's Day to you.**
**Happy Father's Day to you.**
**I'll help you, dear Daddy.**
**Happy Father's Day to you.**

Place a piece of tape on the floor and have children join hands and walk in a circle as they sing. At the end of the song, the child standing nearest the tape must tell some way he or she could help his or her father. This same song could be adapted for Mother's Day.

**58** Sing this action song to the tune of *Twinkle, Twinkle, Little Star.*

**If you're happy, give a clap;**
　Clap hands
**Put your hands back in your lap.**
　Fold hands and place in lap
**If you're happy stomp your feet;**
　Stomp feet
**Stand up tall, then take your seat.**
　Stand, then sit
**If you're happy, show a smile.**
　Draw a smile on your face with your fingertips
**Let's all keep them there a while.**
　Smile broadly for a few moments, then nod to others

**59** Put actions with the words of this song to the tune *Mulberry Bush.*

**This is the way we pick up toys,**
**Pick up toys, pick up toys.**
**This is the way we pick up toys.**
**It's fun to work together.**
**This is the way we open the door,**
**Open the door, open the door.**
**This is the way we open the door.**
**It's fun to work together.**

Let children suggest other verses.

**60** These words fit the tune *Row, Row, Row Your Boat.*

**Help, help, help your friend.**
**Help your friend today.**
**Helping, helping, helping, helping,**
**Helping is the way!**

**61** Use these words and actions to *The Farmer in the Dell.*

**My mother helped me walk**
Walk in place
**When I was very small.**
Fold arms to rock baby
**But there are others I can help**
Point to self
**Since I am growing tall.**
Reach high
**When Mother says, "Clean up!"**
**I help pick up my toys.**
Pick up imaginary toys
**When baby brother's sound asleep,**
Lay cheek on hands with palms together
**I don't make any noise.**
Put finger to closed lips

**62** Teach children this action rhyme to *Mary Had a Little Lamb.*

**I am growing, growing, growing.**
Raise hand to three heights
**Learning what I can do.**
Point to head and nod
**So I can be a helper.**
Point to self
**So can you and you.**
Point to two friends

**63** Have the children join hands and walk in a circle as they sing these words to *Twinkle, Twinkle, Little Star.*

**Helping shows our love, you see.**
**I help you, and you help me.**

Put a piece of tape on the floor. When the music stops, ask the child nearest the tape how he or she will help at home this week. Then you could sing the following verses:

**Helping, helping, can't you see?**
**I am helping, look at me.**
**Sweeping, sweeping, sweeping floors,**
**I am sweeping, sweeping floors.**
**Picking, picking, picking up,**
**I am picking, picking up.**

Fit the verses to the ways the children suggest they will help.

**64** Teach children these words and actions to *Twinkle, Twinkle, Little Star.*

**Can you stretch your arms out far?**
Spread arms out wide
**Can you try to reach a star?**
Reach arms up high
**On one foot can you stand?**
Stand on one foot
**Now can you shake both hands?**
Shake both hands vigorously
**Can you touch your sock and shoe?**
Touch stocking and shoe
**Can you whisper, "God loves you"?**
Cup hands around mouth and whisper

**65** Sing these words to the tune *The Farmer in the Dell.* Children may walk in a circle or clap as they sing.

**How can I be good?**
**How can I be good?**
**Jesus helps me every day.**
**He helps me to be good.**
**I can share my toys.**
**I can share my toys.**
**Jesus helps me every day.**
**He helps me to be good.**
**I help when I forgive.**
**I help when I forgive.**
**Jesus helps me every day.**
**He helps me to be good.**

**66** This action song can be sung to the tune of *Ten Little Indians*.

**Brown hair, red hair,**
    Point to hair
**Blue eyes, green eyes.**
    Point to eyes
**Big feet, small feet,**
    Point to feet
**Short or taller.**
    Touch ground, then reach high
**Jump for joy and**
    Jump
**Clap your hands 'cause**
    Clap
**Jesus loves us all!**
    Arms wide, palms up, then hug self

**67** Sing the following words to the tune of *London Bridge*. Help children join hands and walk in a circle as they sing. They should stop walking on the last line and do the actions for the words they are singing.

**I can learn to help at home,**
**Help at home, help at home.**
**I can learn to help at home.**
**I can pick up toys.**

Ask children to tell other ways they can help at home. Have that become the last line of the song. Other suggestions are holding the door, washing hands, zipping coats, or giving hugs.

**68** Play *London Bridge Is Falling Down*. When the bridge comes down and catches someone, that person's name will be used in the last line of the song. That child must then name his or her favorite food.

**Tell us what you like to eat,**
**like to eat, like to eat.**
**Tell us what you like to eat. (Johnny) tell us.**

Other verses you might use are:

**Tell us what you like to do.**
**Tell us what's your favorite toy.**

**69** This action rhyme may be sung to the tune *Ten Little Indians*.

**I can walk like a tail giraffe.**
    Walk on tiptoes with neck stretched high
**I can hop like a kangaroo.**
    Hop
**I can be kind to everyone as**
    Point to self
**Jesus wants me to.**
    Arms wide, big smile

**70** Words are sung to *The Farmer in the Dell*. You can use a variety of activities while singing these words. The children might keep time with rhythm instruments, march in a circle, clap in time, or walk in pairs around the room.

**God gives us all our food.**
**God gives us all our food.**
**He made the plants and trees for us.**
**God gives us all our food.**
**The farmer grows the food.**
**The farmer grows the food.**
**He takes care of the plants and trees.**
**The farmer grows the food.**
**The cow gives us milk.**
**The cow gives us milk.**
**Hi ho, the dairy-o,**
**The cow gives us milk.**
**We buy our food in stores.**
**We buy our food in stores.**
**Vegetables and fruit to eat.**
**We buy our food in stores.**

**71** The tune *Mulberry Bush* can be used for many actions. The children will enjoy suggesting verses to sing and act out.

**This is the way I put on my hat,**
**Put on my hat, put on my hat.**
**This is the way I put on my hat**
**To come to Sunday School.**
Other possible verses are:

**This is the way we wash our hands.**
**This is the way we iron our clothes.**

## Songs About Friends

**72** Join hands and walk in a circle with your pupils as you sing these words together to the tune of *Farmer in the Dell.*

**I'm looking for a friend.**
**I'm looking for a friend.**
**Oh, will you be my friend today?**
**I'm looking for a friend.**

**73** Children join hands and stand in a circle around you. Sing these words to the tune *Did You Ever See a Lassie:*

**I'm looking for a friend**
**A friend, a friend.**
**I'm looking for a friend**
**To talk to me now.**

Choose a pupil to stand in the middle with you. Shake her hand and say, "How are you, (Christy)?" Encourage the pupil to reply, "I'm fine. How are you?" You step out of the circle and allow the pupil to choose a friend to stand in the circle. Continue the game until every child has been chosen.

**74** Sing the following action rhyme to the tune *Happy Birthday.*

**I know Jesus loves you.**
　　Point to friend
**I know Jesus loves me.**
　　Point to self
**So we'll love one another**
　　Hug self
**In God's family.**
　　Join hands to form circle

**75** Sing the following words to the tune *Mary Had a Little Lamb.*

**God gave me some special friends,**
　　Point up; to self; then to a friend
**Special friends, special friends,**
　　Point to several friends
**God gave me some special friends,**
**And I love them so.**
　　Hug self

**76** Have children join hands with a friend and walk together around the room as they sing these words to the tune *The Farmer in the Dell.*

**I'm glad that you're my friend.**
**I'm glad that you're my friend.**
**Walk with me and talk with me.**
**I'm glad that you're my friend.**

**77** Sing these words to the tune *Twinkle, Twinkle, Little Star.*

**When you're happy, I am, too.**
　　Point to another child and then to self
**When I have a treat, I'll share with you.**
　　Pretend to give something with one hand and eat with the other
**When you're sick, I feel sad.**
　　Hold palm to forehead and then frown
**We're such good friends.**
　　Hold hands with another child
**Aren't you glad?**
　　Smile and nod head
**When you're happy, I am too.**
　　Point to another child and then to self
**You're my good friend;**
　　Shake hands with other child
**I like you.**
　　Point to self, put both hands on heart, then point to other child

**78** Teach your pupils the following song to the tune of *Farmer in the Dell.* They can sing it to their friends at home, too.

**Oh, let's be friends today,**
**Oh, let's be friends today.**
**Let's run and skip and jump and play.**
**Oh, let's be friends today.**

Pupils may join hands in a circle. Sing the song going around the circle one way, then the other.

**79** Ask children to join hands in a circle. Choose a pupil to stand in the middle of the circle. As children walk around in the circle, sing the following words to the tune *Are You Sleeping?*

We are friends. We are friends.
I like you. I like you.
Come and play with me.
Come and play with me.
We are friends. We are friends.

The child in the middle should point to a friend while "I like you" is being sung. The friend should also come to the middle of the circle. Now give a direction to the two friends-something they can do together while holding hands such as jump, skip, or hop around the circle, touch toes ten times, etc.

A variation of this song uses these words:

I'm your friend, I'm your friend.
Come and play, come and play.
I will share with you, I will share with you.
I'm your friend, I'm your friend.

**80** This song is a variation of *The Farmer in the Dell.* Pick one pupil (maybe one that might not be chosen by other children) to be in the middle while other pupils join hands and walk in a circle around him or her. They sing as they walk.

I'm glad that you're my friend,
I'm glad that you're my friend,
Count to three, and stand by me,
I'm glad that you're my friend.

The pupil in the middle picks a friend to come in the middle with him or her. The friend says, "One, two, three," and steps or jumps into the middle. The game continues with the second child picking a friend from the circle, and so on. Soon your circle won't be big enough to fit around all the people in the middle. Start over and play the game enough times so everyone gets a chance to be in the middle.

**81** This song teaches your pupils some important things. The word "forgive" is difficult for young children to understand. Explain that it's like saying "That's okay" to someone who has done something that hurt you. Teach children the following words to the tune *Mulberry Bush.* They can join hands and walk in a circle as they sing.

Jesus helps me say "I'm sorry."
Say "I'm sorry", say "I'm sorry."
Jesus helps me say "I'm sorry."
When I've hurt someone.
Jesus helps me say "I forgive,"
Say "I forgive," say "I forgive."
Jesus helps me say "I forgive,"
When someone hurts me.

**82** Another song about forgiveness can be sung to *Mary Had a Little Lamb.*

Jesus wants me to forgive,
To forgive, to forgive.
Jesus wants me to forgive,
He has forgiven me.

**83** Teach the following words to the tune *The Farmer in the Dell.* Children can sway back and forth or clap their hands as they sing.

Oh, don't be mad at me.
Oh, don't be mad at me.
Let's share our toys and play.
Oh, don't be mad at me.

Then a friend might answer back:

Oh, I'm not mad at you.
Oh, I'm not mad at you.
Let's share our toys and play.
Oh, I'm not mad at you.

**84** Select a child to stand in the center. Have pupils join hands and walk in a circle around him. Sing the following words to the tune *Mulberry Bush*, using the name of the child inside the circle.

(Andy) is a friend of mine,
Friend of mine, friend of mine.
(Andy) is a friend of mine,
And I love him so.

After each child has had a turn to stand inside the circle, sing:

Jesus is a Friend of ours,
A Friend of ours, a Friend of ours.
Jesus is a Friend of ours.
And we love Him so.

**85** Sing the following words to the tune of *Three Blind Mice*.

My friend fell down.
 First child stoops down
My friend fell down. What can I do?
 Second child shrugs shoulders, lifts hands in a question gesture
What can I do? I can be kind and help him up.
 Second child reaches down to help first child up
I can be kind and help him up.
That's what Jesus would want me to do.
It's good to be kind.

Sing the song again with the partners switching roles. Younger children may not learn the words but they will enjoy doing the motions.

**86** Have children join hands and stand in a circle. Teach them the following words to *Mulberry Bush:*

You and I will be kind today,
Be kind today, be kind today.
You and I will be kind today,
So early in the morning.
Place a wide strip of tape at some point outside the circle. As children sing, have them walk around in a circle. At the end of the song, they stop walking, and whoever is standing next to

the tape will tell one way he or she can be kind.

Here is a variation of this song, including actions for several verses.

You and I will be kind today,
Be kind today, be kind today.
You and I will be kind today,
We will listen. Point to ears
We will pick up toys.
 Pretend to pick up toys
We will say kind things.
 Turn to child next to you, and say, "I like you"
We will help at home.
 Ask children to mention ways they can help at home
To everyone we see.
 Shade eyes with hand and look around room

**87** Teach your pupils these words and actions. Sing them to the chorus of *Jesus Loves Me*.

Yes, Jesus loves you.
 Point to friend
Yes, Jesus loves me.
 Point to self
So we love each other
 Hug self
In God's family
 Join hands to form circle

**88** Children might accompany themselves with rhythm instruments as they sing this song to *The Farmer in the Dell*. If they don't use instruments, have them point up on the word "God," to self on the word "me," and to others on the word "you."

I'm glad that God made me,
I'm glad that God made me.
God loves me very, very much,
I'm glad that God made me.
I'm glad that God made you,
I'm glad that God made you.
God loves you very, very much,
I'm glad that God made you.

## Songs About Christmas and Easter

**89** These words are sung to *Mulberry Bush.* Children may clap, or use rhythm instruments as they sing. Shaking jingle bells would be special for them. Remind children that Bethlehem is the town where Jesus was born and shepherds are people who take care of sheep.

Jesus was born In Bethlehem,
In Bethlehem, in Bethlehem.
Jesus was born in Bethlehem,
Born on Christmas Day.
The shepherds went to see Him there,
To see Him there, to see Him there.
The shepherds went to see Him there,
To see the baby Jesus.
The Wise Men brought their gifts to Him,
Their gifts to Him, their gifts to Him.
The Wise Men brought their gifts to Him
And worshiped baby Jesus.

**90** Teach children these words and actions to the chorus of *Jingle Bells.*

Ring the bells, ding-dong-ding;
    Swing arms back and forth
Toot-toot-toot your horn;
    Pretend to blow horn
Trim the tree and hang the star;
    Pretend to hang ornaments on tree
For God's own Son is born!
    Point toward sky

**91** Children will enjoy clapping or using jingle bells while singing these songs. The first one is to *Mary Had a Little Lamb;* the second is to *The Farmer in the Dell.*

Christmas is a happy time,
Happy time, happy time.
Christmas is a happy time,
Because it's Jesus' birthday.

I'm glad that He was born.
I'm glad that He was born.
I'm glad that Jesus came to us.
I'm glad that He was born.

**92** Teach these words and actions to *Brahms' Lullaby (Lullaby and Good-night).*

Little baby so small,
    Bend down
Not much you can do.
    Shake head
Little baby, go to sleep.
    Pretend to rock baby in arms
I'll take good care of you.
    Continue rocking baby, nod head

**93** Sing the following words to *London Bridge Is Falling Down.* When a pupil is "caught" by the "bridge," he or she can tell Mary's news. Children who have been caught can form a "clapping line."

Mary heard some happy news,
Happy news, happy news.
Mary heard some happy news.
Oh, what was it?

**94** Teach children this fun Christmas song to the tune *Ten Little Indians.*

Shh, shh-birds are singing.
    Finger to lips, then flap arms
Shh, shh-mice are creeping.
    Finger to lips, then wiggle fingers
Shh, shh-Mary's rocking.
    Finger to lips, then fold arms
Baby Jesus is sleeping.
    Rest head on hands

**95** Sing the following words to the tune of *Twinkle, Twinkle, Little Star*. Have children raise their arms and open and close their hands to make "twinkling stars."

**Twinkle, twinkle, special star,**
**How I wonder what you are.**
**Up above the world so high,**
**Like a diamond in the sky,**
**Twinkle, twinkle, special star,**
**How I wonder what you are.**
**Twinkle, twinkle, special star.**
**Now I know just what you are.**
**Up above the world so high,**
**Like a diamond in the sky,**
**Twinkle, twinkle, special star,**
**Now I know just what you are!**

**96** This action rhyme is to the tune *Mary Had a Little Lamb*.

**Stars are twinkling overhead**
Wiggle fingers overhead
**As the little grey mouse creeps.**
Wiggle fingers on floor
**In the stable all is still.**
Finger to lips-shhhh
**Baby Jesus sleeps.**
Fold arms and rock baby

**97** Choose one of your pupils to play the part of the shepherd-walking around the inside of the circle, leading another child (his "little sheep") by the hand. Sing the following words to the tune of *Baa, Baa, Black Sheep*.

**Baa, baa little sheep,**
**Come with me.**
**Let's go see what**
**We can see.**
Softly; shepherd and sheep stand still
**Look at the baby**
**Lying in the hay.**
**Little baby Jesus**
**Born this day.**
Joyfully; shepherd and sheep still standing

**That little baby**
**Is God's only Son.**
**Look, oh look**
**At what God's done.**
Eagerly; shepherd and sheep resume walking
**Baa, baa, little sheep,**
**Ring your bell.**
**Let's go see whom**
**We can tell!**

Repeat the song several times, using different shepherds and sheep. If possible, provide a bell for the sheep to ring.

**98** These words fit the tune *Mary Had a Little Lamb*. Place a piece of tape on the floor. Have children join hands and walk in a circle as they sing. When the music stops, the child standing closest to the tape must tell something special about Easter that was learned in class.

**Easter is a happy time,**
**A happy time, a happy time.**
**Easter is a happy time,**
**Jesus is alive.**

**99** Teach children these words and motions to *The Farmer in the Dell*.

**I'm glad for Easter Day!**
Point to self, then clap
**I'm glad for Easter Day!**
**I'm glad that Jesus is alive!**
Clap hands; point finger up
**I'm glad for Easter Day!**

**100** Sing this action song to *The Farmer in the Dell*.

**We all clap and sing.**
Clap
**The stone is rolled away.**
Roll hands one over the other
**Jesus is alive, and He**
Squat, then jump up
**Is with us every day.**
Raise arms and smile

# 100 More Action Songs for Ages 3-5

## Songs About Our World

**1** Let children celebrate the wonderful world God has made as they clap and sing this song to the tune of *The Farmer in the Dell.*

**God gave us a wonderful world.**
**God gave us a wonderful world.**
**Let's all thank Him for this gift.**
**God gave us a wonderful world.**

These next few songs list some of the specific things God has made.

**2** Clap and sing this to the tune of *Row, Row, Row Your Boat:*

**Plants, plants, God made plants.**
**He made all the plants.**
**We need plants to help us live.**
**Praise God for the plants.**

**3** Try to find a picture of each animal mentioned in this song. Hand out pictures and have children hold them up at the appropriate time in the song. Sing to *Paw-Paw Patch.*

**God made lions, God made raccoons.**
**God made dolphins, cats, and baboons.**
**God made birds to sing lots of tunes.**
**God made animals for me and you.**

**God made chicks and kangaroos.**
**God made zebras, dogs, and moose.**
**God made spiders, penguins, too.**
**God made animals for me and you.**

**4** Sing this rhyme to *Skip to My Lou:*

**God made the fish.**
　　Make swimming motions
**And God made the seas.**
**God made the birds.**
　　Make flying motions
**And God made the trees.**
**God made you,**
　　Point to someone
**And God made me.**
　　Point to self
**God made it all.**
　　Spread arms out
**Let's praise Him!**
　　Clap hands

**5** Have children hold hands and sway as they sing this song to *Did You Ever See a Lassie?*

**Did you ever see the oceans,**
**The oceans, the oceans.**
**Did you know God made the oceans?**
**He made them just right.**

Add other verses, substituting words such as "a mountain," "a pear tree," "a parrot," "a zebra," "a snowflake," and so on for the words "the oceans."

## Songs About Jesus and God

**6** Teach children this song which will help them review the creation story. Use motions when appropriate and sing to the tune of *The Farmer in the Dell*.

God said, "I'll make the world." (Repeat)
God said it and the world was made.
God said, "I'll make the world."
God said, "Let there be light." (Repeat)
God said it and the light was made.
God said, "Let there be light."

vs. 3     God said, "I'll make the sky."
vs. 4     God said, "I'll make the seas."
vs. 5     God said, "I'll make the plants."
vs. 6     God said, "I'll make the sun."
vs. 7     God said, "I'll make the moon."
vs. 8     God said, "I'll make the stars."
vs. 9     God said, "I'll make the fish."
vs. 10    God said, "I'll make the birds."
vs. 11    God said, "I'll make the animals."
vs. 12    God said, "I'll make a man."

**7** Here's another creation song to the tune of *Good Night, Ladies*.

God made green trees. (Repeat 2x)
    Pretend to be a tree
I'm glad God made the trees.

God made big whales. (Repeat 2x)
    Pretend to be a whale
I'm glad God made the whales.

God made people. (Repeat 2x)
    Point to each other
I'm glad that God made me.

God made all things. (Repeat 2x)
    Hold arms out to the side
I'm glad God made all things.

**8** *I've Been working on the Railroad* is the tune for this song about Jesus' care.

I'm so glad that Jesus loves me,
    Point up then to self
He helps me each day.
I'm so glad that Jesus loves me,
    Point up then to self
And He never goes away.
    Shake head, "no"
When I'm sad or when I'm lonely,
    Show expressions
When I feel okay-
Jesus loves me and protects me
    Hug self
Every single day.

**9** Children will enjoy helping to make up verses for this next song sung to *The Farmer in the Dell*. Have them point to the things they sing about.

God gives us many things.
God gives us many things.
He gives us all the things we need.
God gives us many things.

The flowers and the trees.
The flowers and the trees.
God gives us all the things we need.
The flowers and the trees.

**10** Sing the verses of the song to *Skip to My Lou*. Do the actions indicated. Add other verses by using different actions for the word "clap" such as "march," "jump," "hop," and "shout."

I love Jesus, yes, I do.
I love Jesus, yes, I do.
I love Jesus, yes, I do.
I love to sing and praise Him.
I love to praise Him with a clap. (Repeat 2 x)
I love to sing and praise Him.

**11** *Mary Had a Little Lamb* is the tune for this next song.

**Are you sick, alone, or sad?**
**Jesus cares, Jesus cares.**
   Point up on the word Jesus
**Are you sick, alone, or sad?**
**Jesus cares for you.**
   Point up then to a person

**12** *The Mulberry Bush* is the tune for this next song. Have children clap as they sing the first verse.

**Jesus is my special friend,**
**Special friend, special friend.**
**I can do things Jesus did.**
**He is my special friend.**

**I can pray like Jesus did,**
**Like Jesus did, like Jesus did.**
**I can pray like Jesus did.**
   Bow heads and fold hands
**He is my special friend.**
   Point up then hug self

**I can tell of Jesus' love,**
**Jesus' love, Jesus' love.**
   Point to mouth then up
**I can tell of Jesus' love.**
**He is my special friend.**
   Point up then hug self

**13** Teach children this song to the tune of *I'm a Little Teapot.*

**Jesus is my best friend**
   Point up
**Yes, indeed!**
   Shake head, "yes"
**He takes care of all my needs.**
**When I am afraid He comforts me.**
   Hug self
**Jesus is my best friend**
   Point up
**Yes, indeed!**
   Shake head, "yes"

**14** Children will enjoy this song which has a different set of actions for each verse. Sing to the tune of *The Muffin Man.*

Stand in a circle and clap to rhythm of words as you sing:
**The children of God needed help,**
**Needed help, needed help.**
**The children of God needed help,**
**To cross the big Red Sea.**

Make sweeping hand motions to show (deep) and (wide):
**The water was deep, the water was wide,**
**Deep and wide, deep and wide.**
**The water was deep, the water was wide.**
**How could they get across?**

Do the actions mentioned in this next verse:
**Did they jump or swim or fly**
**Swim or fly, swim or fly?**
**Did they jump or swim or fly?**
**How did they get across?**

Pretend to blow and sway from side to side. Show path with hands:
**God blew the water from side to side,**
**Side to side, side to side.**
**God blew the water from side to side.**
**So they could get across.**

March in a circle and clap as you sing:
**They walked across like a big parade,**
**A big parade, a big parade.**
**They walked across like a big parade.**
**God helped them get across.**

**15** Lead children in doing the motions for this next song sung to the tune of *The Farmer in the Dell.*

Form roof over head with hands as you sing:

**God gives me a place to live.** (Repeat)
**A happy place that I call home,**
**God gives me a place to live.**

Extend arms as if to hug family as you sing:

**God gives me a family.** (Repeat)
**They always take good care of me, God gives me a family.**

Pretend to throw a ball and then sweep with a broom as you sing:

**We play and work together.** (Repeat)
**Thank You, God, for every day,**
**We play and work together.**

Jump up and down and clap as you sing:

**We praise God for our homes.** (Repeat)
**It's good to have a place to live.**
**We praise God for our homes.**

**16** Sing this song to the tune of *Oh, Be Careful.* Have children stand in a circle and clap to the rhythm of the words, or march around in a circle.

**God gives us everything that we need.**
**God gives us everything that we need.**
**We have a place to stay.**
**We live at home each day.**
**God gives us everything that we need.**

For more verses substitute these lines for the last three of verse one:

vs. 2 **Our friends are happy here.**
**And we're glad to have them near.**
**God gives us everything that we need.**

vs. 3 **He listens as we speak,**
**And He helps us every week.**
**God gives us everything that we need.**

vs. 4 **We listen to Him say,**
**"Obey My rules today."**
**God gives us everything that we need.**

**17** While singing this song let children call out ways Jesus shows His love for them at the end of each verse. Sing to the tune of *The Mulberry Bush.*

**Jesus shows His love for me**
Point to the sky
**Every day, every day.**
Cross arms over chest
**Jesus shows His love for me**
Point to the sky
**In this special way.**
Shake finger in rhythm

**18** For this song, have children join hands and move around in a circle. On the last line, stop and raise up hands, as if pointing to God. Sing to the tune of *The Mulberry Bush.*

**Every time we sing God's praise,**
**Sing God's praise, sing God's praise,**
**Every time we sing God's praise,**
**We show our love to Him.**

**Every time we thank our God,**
**Thank our God, thank our God,**
**Every time we thank our God,**
**We show our love to Him.**

**Every time that we obey,**
**We obey, we obey,**
**Every time that we obey,**
**We show our love to Him.**

**Every time we trust God's care,**
**Trust God's care, trust God's care,**
**Every time we trust God's care,**
**We show our love to Him.**

## Songs About Bible Friends

**19** Children will be reminded of God's care for them by singing these words to the tune of *The Mulberry Bush.* They may enjoy circling around as they sing the first three lines, then stopping and pointing to self on the last line.

God took care of Moses' friends,
Moses' friends, Moses' friends.
God took care of Moses' friends,
And God will care for me.

God took care of Abraham,
Abraham, Abraham.
God took care of Abraham,
And God will care for me.

**20** Teach these words about Peter and John to the tune of *The Mulberry Bush.*

Pretend to walk as you sing:
Peter and John met a man
Met a man, met a man.
Peter and John met a man
On their way to church.

Sit and put on a sad face as you sing:
The man just sat he could not walk
Could not walk, could not walk.
The man just sat-he could not walk.
He was so very sad.

Stand and motion to the sick man as you sing:
Peter and John said, "Rise and walk,
Rise and walk, rise and walk."
Peter and John said, "Rise and walk
In Jesus' name today."

Imitate the man walking happily as you sing:
The man stood up and walked around
Walked around, walked around.
The man stood up and walked around.
He was so very glad!

**21** These words to *Twinkle, Twinkle, Little Star* tell of some of Jesus' miracles. Add actions where appropriate.

Bartimaeus could not see.
Ten men were sick with leprosy.
One was lame and couldn't walk.
One was deaf; one couldn't talk.
Jesus healed them every one
For He was God's only Son.

**22** Review some of the characters of the Old Testament by singing this song to *Are You Sleeping?*

Where is Noah, where is Noah?
Here I am. Here I am.
   Point to self
I will build the ark.
   Pretend to build
I will build the ark.
I'll obey, I'll obey.
   Point to self
Where is Moses, where is Moses?
Here I am. Here I am.
   Point to self
I will lead your people.
   Pretend to walk
I will lead your people.
I'll obey, I'll obey.
   Point to self
Where is Jonah, where is Jonah?
Here I am. Here I am.
   Point to self
I will warn the people.
   Put hand up to mouth
I will warn the people.
I'll obey, I'll obey.
   Point to self
Where are the children? Where are the children? Here we are. Here we are.
   Spread out arms
We will follow Jesus.
   Shake head,"yes"
We will follow Jesus.
We'll obey, We'll obey.

## Songs About Church and Sunday School

**23** Adapt *Old MacDonald Had a Farm* and teach these words that tell about Noah. Add as many animals as you'd like.

**Noah sailed his great big ark**
> Hold two hands together and move like a boat going through water

**Forty days and nights.**
**And on the ark he had two cows,**
> Hold up two fingers

**Forty days and nights.**
**With a moo-moo here, and a moo-moo there,**
> Turn head to right then to left

**Here a moo, there a moo,**
**Everywhere a moo-moo.**
> Spread arms out

**Noah sailed his great big ark**
**Forty days and nights.**

**24** Sing this song to *Baa, Baa, Black Sheep.*

**Little lost sheep, tell me where you are.**
> Put hand to eyes as if looking for the sheep

**Please don't wander very far.**
**It is dark and very cold.**
> Hug self and shiver

**Please come back into the fold.**
> Move hand towards self as if motioning someone to come

**25** This song will remind children to be thankful for leaders that work in their churches. Follow the actions and sing to *Jim Crack Corn.*

**Praise the Lord and walk around,** (Repeat 2x)
**For leaders in our church.**
**Praise the Lord and clap your hands,** (Repeat 2x)
**For teachers in our church.**
**Praise the Lord and jump right up,** (Repeat 2x)
**For the pastor in our church.**
**Praise the Lord and la-la-la,** (Repeat 2x)
Cup hands around mouth on "la-la-la"
**For the choir director in our church.**
Repeat first verse again.

**26** Have children clap as they sing this action song to the tune of *If You're Happy.*

**If you love the Lord your God with all your heart, say I do!** (Repeat)
**You can worship God today,**
**Singing songs will help you say,**
**That you love the Lord your God with all your heart.**

Substitute these lines for the third line above:

**Bringing gifts will help you say ...**
**Offering prayers will help you say ...**
**Clapping hands will help you say ...**
**Shouting praise will help you say ...**

**27** Children will enjoy learning this good-bye song to the tune of *Did You Ever See a Lassie?*

On this first verse, children stand in a circle while leader stands in the middle. On other verses a child can be invited to stand in the middle with the leader.

**Now it's time to say good-bye, good-bye, good-bye,**
**Now it's time to say good-bye, good-bye to our friends.**
**Wave to this friend and that friend,**
     Children wave to each other
**And this friend and that friend.**
**Now it's time to say good-bye, good-bye to our friends.**

**vs. 2 Now it's time to give a hug, a hug, a hug,**

**vs. 3 Next week we'll get together, together, together,**
**Next week we'll get together, together with friends.**
**With this friend and that friend,**
     Children point to each other
**And this friend and that friend.**
**Next week we'll get together, together with friends.**

**28** Use this song to prepare children for the Bible lesson of the day. It is sung to *This Old Man.*

**Listening ears, listening ears,**
     Cup hands behind one ear then the other
**We've all got our listening ears.**
     Cup hands behind both ears
**We will listen to the Word of God today,**
**Hear it and then go obey.**

**29** Lead children in this song about prayer sung to the tune of *This Old Man.*

**We can pray Every day!**
**God will hear us when we say,**
     Fold hands
**"Bless my family and thank You for my food. God is great and God is good."**
**We can pray**
**Every day!**
**Here or there or far away.**
     Fold hands
**"Thank You, God, for going with me everywhere."**
**"Thank You for your loving care."**
     Hug self

**30** Teach children about giving through this song, sung to *The Bear Went Over the Mountain.*

Raise hands, palms up as you sing:
**We bring our offering to church, (Repeat 2x)**
**Because we love our God.**
     Pretend to give an offering as you sing:
**We give our offering to worship, (Repeat 2x)**
**Because we love our God.**

**31** Children will enjoy marching with a partner as they sing these words to *Row, Row, Row Your Boat.*

**Sing, sing, sing to God**
**Praise Him for this day.**
**Happily, happily, happily, happily**
**Praise Him for this day.**

**32** Use this song to the tune of *B-I-N-G-O* to remind children to thank God for His blessings.

Have children clap out the rhythm as they sing this next line:
**T-H-A-N-K, T-H-A-N-K, T-H-A-N-K,**
**So I will thank and praise Him.**

**33** This next song will remind children that God hears them when they pray. It is sung to *The Mulberry Bush.*

**Jesus hears us when we pray,**
**When we pray, when we pray.**
  Cup hand behind ear; make praying hands
**Jesus hears us when we pray.**
**We can pray today.**

**Jesus hears when _____(child's name) prays,**
  Cup hand behind ear; make praying hands.
**_____(child's name) prays, _____(child's name) prays**
**Jesus hears when _____ (child's name) prays,**
**Each and every day.**

**Let's thank God for answered prayer,**
  Point up; make praying hands
**Answered prayer, answered prayer.**
**Let's thank God for answered prayer,**
  Point up; make praying hands
**We can thank Him now.**

**34** Lead children into the activities of the day by singing this song to *Twinkle, Twinkle, Little Star.*

**Hello! How are you today?**
**Would you like to come and play?**
**We will sing and play with toys,**
**With the other girls and boys.**
**We will have a lot of fun!**
**Jesus loves us, every one!**

**35** Children will enjoy doing the motions for this next action song which is sung to *Mary Had a Little Lamb.*

Stand in a circle and clap hands as you sing:
**Little children, praise the Lord,**
**Praise the Lord, praise the Lord.**
**Little children, praise the Lord,**
**Praise the Lord today.**

vs. 2 Open hands, palms facing up for the word "Bible":
**Praise Him for the Bible ...**

vs. 3 Make a triangle-raise arms, hands together, fingers pointing up-for steeple:
**Praise Him for the children's church ...**

vs. 4 Pretend to give an offering:
**Praise Him with our offerings**

vs. 5 Children hold hands and move around in a circle:
**Little children, praise the Lord,**
**Praise the Lord, praise the Lord.**
**Little children, praise the Lord,**
**Praise Him every day.**

**36** *The Itsy Bitsy Spider* is the tune for these words.

**The Bible says God loves us**
  Hold hands together to look like an open book
**He hears our every prayer.**
  Cup hand behind ear
**We praise His name because we know He really cares.**
  Hug self
**We try to love each other; we're learning to forgive.**
  Each child holds another child's hand
**For we want to be like Jesus. Yes!**
**That's the way to live.**
  Shake head, "yes"

**37** Have children hold hands with a partner and sway as they sing this song as an invitation to prayer time. Sing it to *London Bridge.*

**Lord, I like to talk to You,**
**Talk to You, talk to You.**
**Lord, I like to talk to You,**
**When I pray.**

**I love You for all You do,**
**All You do, all You do.**
**I love You for all You do**
**For me each day.**

**Bless my friends and neighbors, too,**
**Neighbors, too, neighbors, too.**
**Bless my friends and neighbors, too.**
**And guide their way.**

**38** Lead children around the room as you sing this song to *The Farmer in the Dell*.

Come worship now with me.
Come worship now with me.
We'll have fun and worship, too.
Come worship now with me.

**39** This song tells of things we do at church. Children will enjoy clapping to the rhythm of this song sung to the tune *She'll Be Comin' Round the Mountain*.

We will learn of Jesus when we
come to church. (Repeat)
We will learn that Jesus loves us. (Repeat)
We will learn of Jesus when we
come to church.

vs. 2 We will read the Bible when we
come to church. (Repeat)
We will read that Jesus loves us. (Repeat)
We will read the Bible when we
come to church.

vs. 3 We will pray together when we come to
church. (Repeat)
We will pray for one another. (Repeat)
We will pray together when we come to
church.

**40** Have children fold their hands as they sing these word to *Twinkle, Twinkle, Little Star*.

When I talk to God I say
"Dear God, help me to obey;
Help me learn to share my toys
With the other girls and boys."
When I talk to God I say,
"Dear God, help me to obey."

**41** *Go In and Out of the Window* is the tune for this next song. Have children divide up into groups of four and join hands. Each of these small groups will circle around during the first part of the song, then move to the center on the last line.

Let's worship God together, (Repeat 3x)
And offerings gladly bring.
Let's tell Him that we're thankful, (Repeat 3x)
And joyful praises sing.
Let's show Him that we love Him; (Repeat 3x)
He gave us everything.
Let's tell the world about Him, (Repeat 3x)
For He's our heavenly King.

## Songs About Family and Friends

**42** This song will remind children to be thankful for their families. Have them clap and sing to the tune of *Jingle Bells*.

Thank You, God; thank You, God,
For my family.
Mother, father, sister, brother,
That You gave to me.
Grandmas, grandpas, uncles, aunts,
Lots of cousins, too.
For this happy family,
Dear God, I do thank You!

**43** Sing these words to the tune of *Did You Ever See a Lassie?*

Oh, I really love my family, my family, my family.
    Point to self, hug self, and sway
Oh, I really love the family that God gave to me;
    Point to self, hug self, point up, and to self
My father and mother and sister and brother.
    Hold up fingers for each person
Oh, I really love the family that God gave to me.
    Point to self, hug self, point up, and to self

**44** You may need some old hats for children to wear during the different verses of this song. Boys can wear men's hats during the "daddy" verse and girls can wear ladies' hats during the "mommy" verse. Sing to the tune of *The Muffin Man*.

Families are a gift from God,
A gift from God, a gift from God.
Families are a gift from God,
Who gives us all good things.

vs. 2 Daddies are a gift from God.
vs. 3 Mommies are a gift from God.

**45** *Three Blind Mice* is the tune for these words about loving our friends. Assign each child a partner and have them face each other as they sing.

We can love.
We can love.
All of our friends, all of our friends.
We can forgive them, and we can share.
Oh, when we are friendly, they'll know we care.
Jesus loves us so much that there's love to spare.
Yes, we can love.

**46** For the first verse of this song, sung to *The Mulberry Bush*, children walk around in a circle holding hands.

We are in a circle of friends,
A circle of friends, a circle of friends.
We are in a circle of friends,
Doodle-lee, doodle-lee, doo!

Children point to themselves then to a friend as they sing:

God loves me and God loves you,
God loves you, God loves you.
God loves me and God loves you,
Doodle-lee, doodle-lee, doo!

Children hug friends standing next to them and sing:

I can hug you when you're sad,
When you're sad, when you're sad.
I can hug you when you're sad.
Doodle-lee, doodle-lee, doo!

**47** This song reminds children in a cheerful way of some of the important things Jesus wants His followers to do. Sing it to the tune of *Did You Ever See a Lassie?* Let children hold hands and sway back and forth gently to the rhythm as they sing.

Let us love one another,
One another, one another.
Let us love one another,
For loves comes from God.
We'll love and forgive
And we'll help and we'll share things.
Let us love one another,
For love comes from God.

**48** Have children hold hands with a partner and swing arms as they sing these words to the tune of *London Bridge.*

Love your friends at all times,
All times, all times.
Love your friends at all times,
This will make God happy.

**49** Children will enjoy the actions in this song sung to the tune of *Twinkle, Twinkle, Little Star.*

I'm so glad that we can be
    Clap in rhythm
Friends together—you and me.
    Clasp hands, point to friend, then to self
Jesus loves you, this I know
    Point up, tap head
For the Bible tells me so.
    Put open hands together like book
I'm so glad that we can be
    Clap in rhythm
Friends together-you and me.
    Clasp hands, point to friend, then to self

**50** Lead children in this action song sung to *The Farmer in the Dell.*

My good friend taps my back.
My good friend taps my back.
We turn around and then sit down.
My good friend taps my back.

vs.2 My good friend shakes my hand ...
vs.3 My good friend smiles at me ...

**51** This friend song is sung to *A Tisket, A Tasket.*

I love you, I love you.
    Pat-a-cake with a friend

You are my friend I love you.
I'll share with you
    Grab hands and swing aims
Be kind to you.
You are my friend, I love you.

**52** *Here's another song about friends to Twinkle, Twinkle, Little Star.*

I just love to run and play
    Run in place
With my special friends each day.
    Point to another child
When I'm sick or feeling sad,
    Hold stomach; frown
Special friends help make me glad.
    Point to other children; smile
I just love to run and play
    Run in place
With my special friends each day.
    Point to another child

**53** For this song, children stand in a circle, holding hands. One child stands in the middle of the circle. Children should walk around while singing the first verse. All verses will be sung to the tune *The Farmer in the Dell*.

**Let's tell all our friends, (Repeat)**
**Tell them Jesus loves them so,**
**Let's tell all our friends,**

The child in the middle should choose a friend to also stand in the circle while this next verse is sung. Name of the child choosing should be inserted in blank below.

_____ (Child's name) **tells a friend.** (Repeat)
_____ (Child's name) **tells of Jesus' love.**
_____ (Child's name) **tells a friend.**

Child chosen during the above verse should then choose another friend to join in circle. Insert that child's name in verse. The last child to be called into the middle should choose a friend to skip with around the other children while the first verse is repeated.

**54** During this song, have children shake hands with each other on the first two lines, then clap hands on the last two. Sing to the tune of *The Farmer in the Dell*.

**I'm glad that you're my friend.**
**Can I be your friend, too?**
**Let's love each other joyfully,**
**And love our God, too!**

**55** Help children to express thankfulness for their friends and families as they sing this song to *We Wish You a Merry Christmas* (chorus only).

Have children hug each other as they sing:

**Let's all love one another.** (Repeat 2x)
**Just like Jesus said.**
Have children join hands as they sing:
**Let's all care for one another.** (Repeat 2x)
**Just like Jesus said.**
Have children walk in a circle as they sing:
**Let's all pray for one another.** (Repeat 2x)
**Just like Jesus said.**

**56** Sing this song about friends to *Mary Had a Little Lamb*. Children clap hands as they sing:

**Jesus gave us friends to love,**
**Friends to love, friends to love.**
**Jesus gave us friends to love,**
**And He loves us, too.**
**I love you and you love me,**
    Children point to another, then to self
**You love me, you love me.**
    Point to self
**I love you and you love me,**
**And Jesus loves us, too.**
    Point up
**Jesus is a friend of mine,**
    Point up, then hug self
**Friend of mine, friend of mine.**
    Hug self
**Jesus is a friend of mine,**
**And I love Him so.**
**I'll help you and you help me,**
    Point to another, then to self
**You help me, you help me.**
    Point to self
**I'll help you and you help me,**
**We can help each other.**

**57** Have children hug themselves, rocking back and forth to the rhythm of this song sung to *London Bridge.* On the last line of each verse they will hug another child.

Jesus is my special friend,
Special friend, special friend.
Jesus is my special friend.
And so are you!

I will love my Je-sus,
Je-sus, Je-sus.
I will love my Je-sus.
And I'll love you, too!

**58** Do the actions mentioned and sing this partner song to *Row, Row, Row Your Boat.*

Love, love, love your friends,
Help to make them smile.
Give your partner one big hug,
And clap your hands awhile.

**59** *I'm a Little Teapot* is the tune for these words about growing up.

Now that I am growing up so tall,
  Crouch down, then reach up high
I can jump a rope, and I can bounce a ball.
  Jump, pretend to bounce a ball
I can help my mother and my dad.
Growing up sure makes me glad.
  Reach up high, stand on tiptoes
I am learning how to sing and pray.
  Cup hands around mouth; fold hands
I am learning how to live God's way.
  Point to self, then up
Learning to be helpful, kind, and true,
Is the best thing I can do!
  Clap on the four major beats

**60** Sing this growing up song to the tune of *Did You Ever See a Lassie?* Pantomime the activity in each verse.

Would you like to be a grown-up,
A grown-up, a grown-up?
God will help you as you grow up,
But what will you do?

I'll cook in the kitchen,
The kitchen, the kitchen.
God will help me as I grow up,
And that's what I'll do.

vs. 2 I'll work in an office...
vs. 3 I'll play with the children
vs. 4 I'll sing praise to Jesus...

**61** Teach these words to *Ten Little Indians.* Add actions when appropriate.

Trees and flowers—watch them grow.
They need sun and rain you know.
God made many things we see.
He made even you and me!

**62** Here's a song about taking care of our pets sung to *Mary Had a Little Lamb*.

I can love my pet today,
Fill his food and water tray.
I will take good care of him.
God will help me.

**63** Do these words to the tune of *Itsy Busy Spider*.

Sharing is for children;
This is how I know.
    Join hands and walk in a circle
A boy shared his lunch
With Jesus long ago.
    Everyone walk toward center of circle,
    hands still joined
This made Jesus happy,
And we can please Him, too,
    Drop hands, clap as you back out of center
    By sharing with each other
As God would have us do.
    Join hands again and walk in a circle

**64** Let pairs of children march around as they sing this sharing song to the tune of *The Mulberry Bush*.

Jesus loves it when we share,
When we share, when we share,
Jesus loves it when we share,
Let's all share today.

**65** This song will remind children that it is pleasing to God when we share. Sing to the tune of *Three Blind Mice*.

I like to share. Clap
I like to share. Clap
I like to share. Clap
I like to share. Clap
All the things God has given to me,
He wants me to share very joyfully.
By sharing I'm like Jesus wants me to be.
Yes, I like to share. Clap
I like to share. Clap

**66** Lead children in clapping and singing these words to *This Old Man*.

God wants us to be fair,
Kind, and helpful,
And to share.
With a great big happy smile,
We can get along.
Clap your hands and sing this song!

**67** Children will be reminded that God made them in this next song sung to *Three Blind Mice*.

God made you. God made me.
    Point to someone, then to self
God made you. God made me.
He made my head, and my knees,
and my toes.
    Point to body parts mentioned
He made my eyes, and my hands,
and my nose.
    Point to body parts mentioned
Because He made me He loves me so.
    Hug self
Yes, God made us all!
    Point up and to others
God made us all!

**68** Teach children this fun song to the tune of *The Farmer in the Dell*.

**We're growing by leaps and bounds.** (Repeat)

> Crouch down and jump up

**Just like Jesus, we're growing up,**
**We're growing by leaps and bounds.**

> Repeat actions

**When Jesus was growing up** (Repeat)

> Start from a crouching position and straighten up a little

**Mary and Joseph took care of Him**
**When Jesus was growing up.**

> Stand up straight

**When Jesus was twelve years old** (Repeat)

> Stand on tip-toes, stretching as tall as possible

**He went to the temple to learn about God**
**When Jesus was twelve years old.**
**The Spirit came to Him.**

> Raise hands up over head and bring back down to touch shoulders, like a dove descending on a person

**When Jesus went to be baptized,**
**The Spirit came to Him.**

> Repeat hand motions

**Just like the fishermen,** (Repeat)

> Pretend to throw out nets and haul them in

**We will come when Jesus calls,**
**Just like the fishermen.**

> Repeat first verse.

**69** After each verse of this song, choose a child to call out something that he/she couldn't do when younger. Sing to the tune of *Are You Sleeping?*

Leader (or group): **Are you growing?**
**Are you growing?**
Children: Yes, I am! Yes, I am!
Leader (or group): **Show us how you're growing.**
**Show us how you're growing.**
**If you can. If you can.**

After several times through, close with this verse:

Leader: **Are you growing? Are you growing?**
Children: Yes, I am! Yes, I am!
Leader: **As your life keeps going,**
**Who can keep you growing?**
Children: Jesus can! Jesus can!

**70** Teach these words to *Jesus Loves the Little Children*.

**Jesus calls the little children,**

> Put hands up to mouth

**Calls us all to follow Him.**
**If we follow Him each day,**

> Pretend to march in place

**We will never lose our way.**
**Jesus calls the little children.**
**"Follow Me!"**

> Put hands to mouth then motion, "follow me"

**71** Children might like to sway as they sing this next song to the tune of *Rock-a-Bye Baby*.

**Who loves the children**
**Black, white, and red?**

> Pat cheeks

**Who loves the children**
**Going to bed?**

> Rest hands on head

**Who loves the children**
**Kneeling to pray?**

> Fold hands in prayer

**God our good Father**

> Point up

**Loves us each day.**

> Hug self

**Who loves the children**
**Both far and near?**

> Indicate left and right

**Who loves the children**
**Calming their fear?**

> One hand strokes the other

**Who loves the children**
**Showing the way?**

> March in place

**God our good Father**

> Point up

**Loves us each day.**

> Hug self

**72** Children will be encouraged by this next song which reminds them that God is with them when they are afraid. Sing to the tune of *Down by the Station.*

**I'm not afraid when Boom! goes the thunder.**
> Clap hands on "boom"

**I'm not afraid when winds blow all around.**
> Wave hands all around

**I remember Jesus is my loving Savior.**
> Point up; cross arms on chest

**Clap, clap, stamp, stamp**

**I'm His child.**

**I'm not afraid when I am feeling lonely.**
> Rest chin in hands

**I'm not afraid when Mommy's not around.**
> Look around

**I remember Jesus is my loving Savior.**
> Point up; cross arms on chest

**Clap, clap, stamp, stamp**

**I'm His child.**

**73** Children will enjoy the clapping part of this song which is sung to the tune of *Hickory, Dickory, Dock.*

**Do you know who loves me?**
> Clap, clap

**Do I know who loves you?**
> Clap, clap

**Our Father God in heaven above**

**Loves you and loves me, too!**
> Clap, clap

**74** Teach children these words and actions to *Mary Had a Little Lamb.*

**Jesus loves you,**
> Point up and to others

**Yes, He does. (Repeat 2x)**
> Nod head

**Jesus loves me,**
> Point up and hug self

**Yes, He does.**
> Nod head

**Jesus, we love You, too.**
> Point up

**75** Teach these words to *Mary Had a Little Lamb.*

**People, people, everywhere**
> Point to people around you

**Everywhere, everywhere.**

**We love people everywhere,**
> Hug self

**Because God made them.**

## Songs About Helping

**76** This is a song that is great to sing while cleaning up. Sing to the tune *Are You Sleeping?*

I am helping, I am helping.
Look at me! Look at me!
Pick up all the paper,
Clean off all the tables,
Nice and neat, nice and neat.

**77** Add actions to this song to the tune of *Ten Little Indians.*

These hands, these hands,
These hands are helping hands.
These hands, these hands,
These hands are helping hands.
These hands, these hands,
These hands are helping hands.
They show Jesus' love.
vs. 2 These feet ...

**78** Teach this helping song to *Mary Had a Little Lamb.*

Have children pretend to pick up paper scraps as they sing:
I can pick up paper scraps,
Paper scraps, paper scraps.
I can pick up paper scraps.
I'm a helper here.

Have children sing in a whisper:
I can listen quietly,
Quietly, quietly.
I can listen quietly.
I'm a helper here.

## Songs About Holidays

**79** Teach this Valentine song to *Three Blind Mice.*

Please be my Valentine.
    Point to self
I'll love you
    Point to another
All the time.
Because Jesus loved me
    Point to self
I love you, too.
    Point to another
Jesus told us to love
For it's right to do.
    Everybody holds hands
Love one another
The whole year through.
So please be my Valentine.

**80** Teach children this Easter praise song to the tune of *Mary Had a Little Lamb.* Have them clap along.

Jesus is God's special Son,
Special Son, special Son.
Jesus is God's special Son.
He's alive!
Let's praise Him!

**81** Letting children play musical instruments with this next Easter song will add to the festivities. Sing to the tune of *Old MacDonald Had a Farm.*

Wake up early!
Shout and sing.
Jesus is alive!
Flowers bloom, and bells all ring.
Jesus is alive!
So clap your hands;
Stamp your feet.
Here a clap, there a clap;
Everywhere a stamp, stamp.
Wake up early!
Shout and sing.
Jesus is alive!

**82** Children will be able to sing about Easter with these words which are sung to *Down by the Station*.

Down in the garden
Early in the morning
Mary saw the cave where
    Hold hands up to eyes as if looking
She thought Jesus lay.
But the stone was gone
And there were angels waiting!
    Point finger as you sing this next line
"Jesus is alive,"
Is what she heard them say.

Mary ran to tell the
Other friends of Jesus
    Pretend to run
That the stone was gone
And Jesus was alive.
Suddenly they saw Him
    Hold hands up to eyes
Standing right beside them.
    Point finger as you sing this next line
He said,
"Peace be with you!"
And they were surprised!

**83** If you have a special Mother's Day program, invite children to make a circle around their mothers and sing this song to *The Farmer in the Dell*.

You're the best mom in the world. (Repeat)
Yes, I really love you so.
You're the best mom in the world.
You take good care of me. (Repeat)
Yes, I really love you so.
You take good care of me.
You teach me how to pray. (Repeat)
Yes, I really love you so.
You teach me how to pray.

Repeat the first verse.

**84** Here's another Mother's Day song to the tune of *Old MacDonald Had a Farm*.

Sing a song about today:
Happy Mother's Day!
    Start to clap hands on the next line
Clap your hands and shout,
"Hooray!" Happy Mother's Day.
So clap your hands, Shout, "Hooray!"
Here a clap, there a shout,
Everywhere we sing about:
Happy, happy Mother's Day,
Happy Mother's Day!

**85** This Father's Day song can be sung by children to their fathers at home or in a program. Sing to *Twinkle, Twinkle, Little Star*.

Daddy, Daddy,
I love you,
    Point to Dad
And the many things you do.
    Put hands on hips
You take care of me each day,
    Point to Dad
Read me books and even play.
    Pretend to read a book
Daddy, Daddy, I love you.
    Point to Dad
Happy Father's Day to you!

**86** This Thanksgiving song is sung to the tune of *Row, Row, Row Your Boat*. After each time of singing, ask children to name something they are thankful for.

Here comes Thanksgiving Day.
Let's all shout, "Hooray!"
Let's thank God for everything
He gives us every day!

**87** Here's another Thanksgiving song to the tune of *Jesus Loves Me*.

**Thank You for the food I eat,**
  Make eating motions
**And for all the friends I meet.**
  Wave to friends
**Thank You for the clothes I wear,**
  Point to clothing
**And for all your love and care.**
  Hug self

**Oh, Jesus, thank You.**
**Oh, Jesus, thank You.**
**Oh, Jesus, thank You.**
**Thank You for everything.**

**88** This last Thanksgiving song is sung to *She'll Be Comin' Round the Mountain When She Comes.*

**Let's all clap because we're thankful for our food.**
Spoken: yum, yum. Rub stomach
**Let's all clap because we're thankful for our food.**

**Let's all clap because we're thankful**
**Let's all clap because we're thankful**
**Let's all clap because we're thankful for our food.**
vs. 2 **Let's all clap because we're thankful for our beds**
Spoken: ahhhh. Pretend to be asleep

vs. 3 **Let's all clap because we're thankful for our clothes**
Spoken: zzzip. Run thumb from waist to chin

**89** Lead children in praising God for sending Jesus by doing this action song sung to the tune of *London Bridge*.

**Who's the child in the manger bed?**
  Hold hands in V shape
**Manger bed, manger bed?**
**Who's the child In the manger bed?**
**Jesus Christ, the Savior!**
  Point up

**Who's the child in Mary's arms?**
  Rock child in arms
**Mary's arms, Mary's arms?**
**Who's the child in Mary's arms?**
**Jesus Christ, the Savior!**
  Point up
**Who did the shepherds find one night?**
  Shield eyes and look around
**Find one night? Find one night?**
**Who did the shepherds find one night?**
**Jesus Christ, the Savior!**
  Point up
**Who did Simeon and Anna see?**
  Cup hands around eyes
**Simeon see? Anna see?**
**Who did Simeon and Anna see?**
**Jesus Christ, the Savior!**
  Point up

**90** Have children follow the actions in this song sung to the tune of *Row, Row, Row Your Boat*.

**Look, look, look and see,**
  Cup hands around eyes; look around
**See what God has done!**
  Spread hands outward
**See the baby in the manger,**
  Rock baby in arms
**He is God's own son.**
  Point upward
**Bow, bow, bow your head,**
  Bow head
**Worship Him today.**
  Bow head and fold hands
**He is Lord and He is King-**
  Raise head and arms upward
**This Baby in the hay.**
  Rock baby in arms
**Come, come, come to Him,**
  Beckon with one hand
**He will show the way.**
  Extend hand; sweep to side
**Jesus is our loving Savior,**
  Hug self
**Born on Christmas Day.**
  Rock baby in arms

**91** Use this as an Advent song by adding a verse each week of Advent. Sing to *Mary Had a Little Lamb.*

**Mary had a baby boy, baby boy, baby boy.**
> Pretend to rock a baby

**Mary had a baby boy, and Jesus was His name.**

**Angels came to tell the news, tell the news, tell the news.**
> Put hands to mouth

**Angels came to tell the news, and Jesus was His name.**

**Shepherds came to visit Him, visit Him, visit Him.**
> Pretend to be shepherds coming to see the baby

**Shepherds came to visit Him, and Jesus was his name.**

**Wise men came to see Him, too, see Him, too, see Him, too.**
> Pretend to be the wise men on camels

**Wise men came to see Him, too, and Jesus was His name.**

**God gave us a precious gift, precious gift, precious gift.**
> Point up

**God gave us a precious gift, and Jesus is His name.**

**92** These words can be sung to the tune of *Twinkle, Twinkle, Little Star.*

**Hello, shepherds! Listen to me**
> Cup hand behind ear

**While I sing this melody.**
> Wiggle fingers like playing a piano

**Jesus Christ is born this day.**
> Point upward

**He is sleeping in the hay.**
> Rock baby in arms

**Hello, shepherds! Run and see!**
> Cup hands around eyes

**Jesus came to you and me.**
> Point to others, then to self

**93** This Christmas song is sung to *Jesus Loves Me.*

> Pretend to rock baby as you sing:

**Mary had a baby boy**
**And her heart was filled with joy.**
**God's own Son is born today**
**In a manger filled with hay.**
> Clap hands and sing the chorus:

**It's Jesus' birthday;**
**It's Jesus' birthday.**
**It's Jesus' birthday, and I thank God for Him.**

**vs. 2 Shepherds heard the angels say,**
> Put hand to ear

**"Jesus Christ is born today.**
> Point finger as you sing

**You'll find Him in Bethlehem."**
> Run in place

**Off they ran to look for Him.**

**94** Teach these words to the tune *Ten Little Indians.*

**Birthday, birthday, someone's birthday!**
**(Repeat 2x)**
**Who can that someone be?**

    Scratch head, shrug shoulders

Insert correct name: **Tommy, Tommy,**
**Tommy's birthday! (Repeat 2x)**
**Let's celebrate-hooray!**

    Clap on last line

Christmas verse:
**Jesus, Jesus, Jesus' birthday! (Repeat 2x)**
**Let's celebrate-hooray!**

    Clap on last line

**95** Let children play rhythm instruments along with this next song which is sung to *Jingle Bells.*

**Happy day!**
**Happy day!**
**Jesus Christ is born!**
**See the Baby in the hay**
**On this bright Christmas morn!**

**Happy day!**
**Happy day!**
**Jesus is God's Son.**
**We can sing and clap-hooray!**
**Oh, see what God has done!**

**96** Children will enjoy moving around and stretching as they sing this song to *If You're Happy.*

**Count to three and stretch your arm—**
**One, two, three!**

    Stretch arm

**Count to three and shake your foot—**
**One, two, three!**

    Shake your foot

**Touch your head and touch your toes.**
**Don't forget to touch your nose.**

    Touch head, toes, nose

**Count to three and now sit down—**
**One, two, three!**

    Sit down

**97** Teach these words and actions to *London Bridge.*

**Reach up high on tippy toes!**
**Praise the Lord!**
**Praise the Lord!**
**Reach up high on tippy toes!**
**Then sit down!**

**Stand and clap your hands for joy!**
**Praise the Lord!**
**Praise the Lord!**
**Stand and clap your hands for joy!**
**Then sit down!**

**98** Do the motions and sing this song to *Twinkle, Twinkle, Little Star.*

Hop on both feet.
Hop on one.
Turn around,
And run, run, run.
  Children run in place
I am happy as can be!
Jesus is a friend to me!
Hop on both feet.
Hop on one.
Turn around
And run, run, run.

**99** For this song have the children make a big circle. One child may march around the circle on the first verse. Add a child to the marching group for each verse. Try to make sure each child gets a chance to march. Sing to the tune *When Johnny Comes Marching Home.*

We go marching one by one, hurrah, hurrah.
We go marching one by one, hurrah, hurrah.
We go marching one by one,
Thanking God for all He's done.
And we all go marching round and round in the praise parade.

vs. 2. We go marching two by two, hurrah, hurrah ...
Thanking God for me and you

vs. 3. We go marching three by three
Thanking God for those who love me ...

vs. 4. We go marching four by four
Thanking God for a whole lot more ...

vs. 5. We go marching five by five
Thanking God that we're alive ...

vs. 6. We go marching six by six
Thanking God for what comes next ...

vs. 7. We go marching seven by seven
Thanking God for making heaven ...

vs. 8. We go marching eight by eight
Thanking God for friends so great ...

vs. 9. We go marching nine by nine
Thanking God for feeling fine ...

vs. 10. We go marching ten by ten
Thanking God for the fun this has been ...

**100** Sing to *The Farmer in the Dell.*

I can stretch up high.
  Stretch arms up
I can squeeze down low.
  Crouch down
I can turn around, and then
  Turn around once
Sit down nice and slow.
  Sit down quietly

# 100 Activities for Ages 3-5

Here are 100 ideas for activities you can do with children in your classroom or at home. Some activities are best suited for two year olds; others will be enjoyed most by four or five year olds. As you do these activities with your children, relate each activity to God's love and all that He does for us.

## Activities About Jesus and God

### 1 Sheepfold

Use this activity when you have a Bible story about Jesus, our Good Shepherd, or young David or any other person who was a shepherd.

Help children make a sheepfold by making a fence of blocks. Leave an open doorway. Place cotton balls inside of the fence for sheep. Move the sheep outside the sheepfold to eat grass: put sheep inside the sheepfold to sleep.

**Option:** Make a sheepfold of chairs: let children be sheep.

### 2 God the Creator

Have children help you look through old magazines and find pictures of things that God made (plants, animals, people). Tear or cut out the pictures and glue them on pieces of paper or grocery sacks.

Lead children in thanking God for His creations. Have a child point to each picture and say, "Thank You, God, for . . ." (name object in picture).

### 3 God Made...

Help children remember some of God's creations by playing a simple version of "Simon Says." After naming one of the many things that God created, do an action with your child. You might say, "God made the fish" as you pretend to swim, and "God made the birds" as you pretend to fly. End your game by saying these words from Genesis 1:31: "Everything God made was very good."

### 4 What Did Adam Need?

Have children imitate you as you act out some of the things Adam needed. Ask: "Who made the things Adam needed?" Then tear out magazine and catalog pictures of things God gives us: homes, food, water, plants, friends. Paste the pictures on construction paper, punch a couple of holes on one side, and tie the pages together with yarn to make a book. Write on the cover, "God Gives Us What We Need."

### 5 Animals in the Ark

Select an animal picture book and help children name animals Noah may have taken into the ark. Talk about how Noah obeyed God by building an ark and taking animals inside.

Children might want to gather stuffed animals. They could pretend to take the animals inside a boat made of chairs. Mention during the week that we obey God just as Noah did when we talk to God, do what Mom and Dad say, show love for others, etc.

### 6 Sharing Like Abraham

Children will enjoy the story of Abraham and Lot if you provide some blocks to build a well and some cotton balls to represent sheep as in the first activity. Help crowd the cotton "sheep" all around the well, then divide them into two groups, as Abraham and Lot divided the land. Talk about how God wants families to get along.

*(Continued on next page.)*

Encourage the beginning of sharing by giving children enough crayons or cookies so they can "share" some and still have plenty. At this point in their growth, just establish that sharing makes everyone happy.

# 7 God Gives Water

When children ask for drinks of water, talk about how God helped Moses and the people have water in the desert. Since we don't get water by hitting rocks, help the children understand that the water from the faucet also comes from God. In a simple way describe how water from rivers and lakes comes into your house through pipes.

Then use some of that water to make lemonade or a fruit drink with a citrus fruit and sugar. As you add the water to your drink, tell children that many of the things we drink contain water.

# 8 King David's Throne Room

When presenting the story about Mephibosheth from 2 Samuel 9, use this role play activity to help children understand the significance of David's actions. This also is a helpful activity to introduce a discussion about disabilities. Help children understand that God made everyone special and He loves each person very much. That includes people with disabilities.

King David wanted to help his friend's family. Jonathan had a son who was lame. David sent Ziba (a man who used to work for Jonathan's family) to bring Mephibosheth, who couldn't walk like most people, to the palace so he could be kind to him.

To play-act this story, use three characters: King David; Ziba the servant; and lame Mephibosheth. To include more children, have people standing around to help King David or attendants to fan him.

Show children how to act when they play the part of Mephibosheth. Walk slowly, dragging one foot along. If some of the children start to giggle, encourage them to be kind.

Since this is a short scene, go through it several times, letting different children take the speaking parts. They will need help the first few times to know what to say.

# 9 Bringing the Offering

To help children learn about the importance of the offering, pretend that you are a Bible-time leader. You could drape a shawl or stole around your neck as the temple helpers did in Bible times. Announce the time for the people (children) to prepare for the offering by saying, "Come to the temple! Put your offering money in the offering box." Place a special container on a table. Use this container for this purpose each Sunday. You may want to act out a portion of the story about King Joash taking offerings to repair the temple (2 Chron. 24:1-14) or a similar passage. Children can put coins in the container for the offering and give just as Joash and the people did.

# 10 Building the Wall

*In advance:* When telling the story of Nehemiah building the wall (see Nehemiah 2), prepare a section of wall or room divider so that it is blank. Give each child a sheet of construction paper in a color contrasting to the blank wall.

Have one child bring his paper and stand in front of the group. Say, "Here is a worker who wants to help build the wall. He has a building block." Have him take his building block and tape it on the wall just above the floor." Then say, "He has done his work and used his building block to build a wall. But his one building block didn't make a whole wall. He doesn't have any blocks left. How can we get a whole wall?" Other children will volunteer to use their building blocks.

Let children tape their blocks, one at a time (like laying bricks), to the wall, adding to those already there. Allow children to "lay" more than one brick, especially if your group is small. When the wall is completed, talk about what a good job was done because everyone worked together.

## 11 Working Together

Here is a variation of the previous activity. Work together to build a wall of blocks or interlocking blocks just as Nehemiah and the people worked together to build a wall around the city of Jerusalem (see Nehemiah 2). Then act out ways people at your church work together: a choir practicing, a class cleaning up a Sunday school room, and so forth. Act out ways families work together such as raking leaves, cleaning up toys.

## 12 Happy Birthday, Jesus

Near Christmastime, print the words "Happy Birthday, Jesus" on a paper for your child to decorate with crayons. (Idea: Put a line of glue along the letters; let child sprinkle with glitter.) Help child hang the paper up as you sing "Happy Birthday" to Jesus several times.

## 13 Water from a Well

When telling a Bible story that refers to a well (Jacob meeting Rachel or the story of Jesus and the woman at the well) demonstrate for children what a well was like. Using toy figures and a large bowl of water, make a "well" by taping string to a small plastic cup and dipping it into the water. Let children take turns hauling water from the well. This simple activity will help them understand the story and what life was like in Bible times.

## 14 I'm Sorry

Use this simple activity to help children understand that Zacchaeus was sorry for his wrong actions. Draw a happy face on one side of a paper plate and a sad face on the other side. As you tell the story in Luke 19:1-10, have children show the side of the plate which matches how Zacchaeus felt. At the end of the story, talk about how happy Zacchaeus felt because Jesus cared for him. End this time by saying a prayer thanking God for loving us even when we do wrong things.

This same activity can be used for any story in which people felt sad and then happy—such as Peter's denial, how Jesus felt when Lazarus died, and so forth.

## 15 Being a Good Samaritan

Tell the story of the good Samaritan from Luke 10:25-37. Pause after telling about each character who saw the hurt man and ask, "Does Jesus want us to be like that person?" Children will imitate your actions as you shake your head and answer "yes" or "no." Let children practice putting plastic bandages on a doll just as the Samaritan helped the hurt man. Then help children think of ways to be good Samaritans at home by doing kind things.

## 16 Bartimaeus Can See!

After telling the story of blind Bartimaeus in Luke 18:35-43, have children use the side of a dark crayon to fill a piece of paper with a dark color. Explain that this is how everything looked to Bartimaeus when he was blind. Then reread the last part of the story. Help children think of things Bartimaeus saw when Jesus healed his eyes. Turn paper over and let children scribble color with bright colors like blue for the sky, yellow for the sun, and green for the grass.

## 17 Jesus Helps Us See

Help children understand more about blindness by playing a game. Show a familiar object such as food or a toy. Ask children to tell you what the object is. Then tell children to close their eyes. Can they see the object now? Can they remember what the object is? Have children open their eyes, and name the object again. (Repeat the game with another item.)

Remind children that Jesus made the blind man able to see by touching his eyes. Jesus cares about all the problems and joys in your child's life.

## 18 Jesus and the Fishermen

In a large basin with an inch or two of water (or at bath time at home), provide some toy boats or fish. You might have fun making boats from meat trays. As children play, talk about how Jesus met some fishermen and went out in a boat with them. If you have a colander, sieve, or a piece of netting to scoop up toys, children will better understand how the fishermen used nets to catch fish. How nice to know that Jesus wanted some fishermen to be His helpers. We can learn to be Jesus' helpers, too.

## 19 Friends Like Jesus

During the preschool years, children need time to develop social skills. A good way to practice is for children to "visit" each other. Help children prepare for a friend's visit just as Mary, Martha, and Lazarus prepared to have their friend Jesus come. Children can help fix a simple snack, lay out the plates and napkins, get out some toys. Talk about the importance of sharing things and how fun it is to get ready for a friend's visit.

## 20 Early Christians

Help children name the things the early Christians did when they met together. (See Acts 1, 2: They prayed and ate, sang and shared.) Point out that these are things which children today do at Sunday school. Older children may enjoy being leaders. They may want to take turns saying brief prayers or suggesting favorite songs. Provide a snack (fruit slices or crackers) that children can thank God for and share together.

You can do these things at home, too. Look for times to give thanks spontaneously with your child. When you enjoy something together, pause in your fun to thank God for all the good times and blessings He has given you. If your extended family or friends gather for a holiday feast, remember to celebrate the way the early Christians did.

## 21 Let's Catch Some Fish

Let children pretend they are Bible-time fishers. Since only nets were used back then to catch fish, this activity will challenge children to try to throw out their nets and haul in some fish the way people did in Jesus' day. Put blue fabric on the floor to represent the water. Then put paper or plastic fish on the water. Make fish nets from coarse fabric netting or from mesh bags in which grocers package potatoes and oranges. Weight the nets to make them easier to throw by taping pennies to the edges.

## 22 God's Rules Make Us Happy

Play a game that reinforces God's rules. Let each child draw a happy face on one side of a paper plate, and a sad face on the other side. Each time you name something God wants us to do, have the child show the happy face. If you name something God doesn't want us to do, have child show the sad face. As you play, explain in simple terms the reasons behind life's do's and don'ts.

## 23 Touch and Taste

Have foods with different textures, shapes, and tastes such as fuzzy peaches, smooth apples, bumpy carrots, and skinny bananas.

**Touch:** To help children concentrate on touch, have them close their eyes and feel the fruit and other foods. Tell children to guess the names of the foods they are feeling.

**Taste:** Cut the fruits or vegetables into small slices and put them on napkins for children to taste. Also encourage them to use their sense of smell to guess what it is.

## 24 Do as I Do

Have children sit down on the floor around you with their eyes closed. Then make sounds as the children listen.

Clap your hands, click your tongue, sing a song, etc. Then ask children to try to figure out how you made the sounds and to try to imitate.

Use objects to make different sounds. For example, bounce a ball and tap toys such as blocks together to make interesting sounds. Then have children open their eyes and point to what you used to make the sounds.

## 25 Shadows

Use a bright light to make shadows in the room. Have children look at their shadows. Are the shadows bigger or smaller than the children are? Can they make the shadows change? How? Notice shadows of other objects. Do they all fall on the same side?

Go outside. Look at shadows of big things-a car or building. Stand on the shadow side, then on the sunny side. What difference do you feel?

## 26 Noise Hunt

God gave us ears for listening. Sit or stand quietly in one place outside and listen to noises. Encourage children to name noises they hear: birds, wind, etc. Try imitating the sounds. Then, if you wish, return inside and make a list of all the noises. Draw pictures of things that made noise.

## 27 Map

Cut out a construction paper church resembling your own church building. Place it in the center of a large sheet of paper or bulletin board. Also cut out a car from an ad or from construction paper. Ask the children on which side of the church building you should park the car. What else needs to go nearby to make this more like "our church"?

After a few questions have been raised, suggest going outside to check. Walk around the church building and let children point out what they should put on the map. Back in the room they may draw and cut out cars, trees, neighboring houses, and other items to complete the map. When the map is finished, thank God for your church. Pray for people in the neighborhood.

## 28 Rock-collecting Walk

Two good things about collecting rocks are: (a) There always seems to be enough for everyone; (b) the children don't spoil any gardeners' work. Just after a rain or at a pond's edge they will find pretty, wet rocks. Put them in jars of water. Other things to do with rocks are:
1. Place them on paper plates according to size, color, or another feature. Make a label for each plate: small rocks, shiny rocks, etc.
 2. Paint eyes and other features to make pet rocks.
3. Lay the rocks in a row in order from small to large, dark to light. Count them.

## 29 Picture Hunt

*In advance:* Cut out pictures of things children enjoy from magazines, newspapers, or toy catalogs. Mount the pictures on construction paper so they will be sturdier. Try to find enough pictures so that there are at least two or three for each child. Hide these pictures around the room.

When children arrive, have them go on a "picture hunt." Each child should stop looking and sit down when he or she has found the limit of two or three pictures. (This will allow everyone to find some.)

Then have children sit in a circle. Ask each child to tell about his or her pictures with the group. Ask simple questions to stimulate conversation.

## 30 Weather Fun

Give each child four 4" x 4" sheets of paper. Help each child make diagonal marks on one for rain; dots on one for snow; a large circle with sun-burst effect for the sun. On the last page put a copy of the following poem for parents to read to them. Fasten the sheets together at one corner with paper fastener. Children can turn from page to page as you repeat this poem:

*Jesus helps me in the rain;*
*Jesus helps me in the snow;*
*Jesus helps me in the sunshine.*
*Jesus is my Friend, I know.*

## 31 Nature Center

As spring approaches, begin a nature center. Use a table or low shelf where children can see and handle the things on display.

Potted plants and flowers in vases are appropriate but don't limit yourself to garden flowers. Wild flowers and even dandelions can be beautiful. Encourage children to bring in things for the center. Treat any contribution as an important creation of God. Look especially for a discarded bird's nest, a branch of new leaves, pussy willows.

As summer approaches children might add shells from a vacation at the beach, little stones from other places they visit, and so on. Remind them not to take things from state and national parks, and not to hurt any growing plant.

Keep changing objects at your nature center to keep interest high. Use items to talk about God's plan for growing things, the seasons, etc.

## 32 Seasons Tree

Put four branches in a pot of sand. Divide children into four groups and assign each a branch to "dress" for a certain season. Use construction paper to make the following:

**Spring:** Small buds and blossoms.

**Summer:** Green leaves and butterflies.

**Fall:** Colored leaves with apples.

**Winter:** Snow (cotton) and maybe a cardinal.

## 33 Follow the Leader

Provide each child with a large sheet of construction paper which has been divided into equal fourths. Explain that you are the leader and they are the followers in this game.

Then draw a square, a circle, a rectangle, or a triangle in any of the four squares. The children must follow the leader by drawing the same shape in the same square on their own paper. If you color the shape, children should color their shape the same color. Repeat this three times, using a different shape in each square. Or choose different children to be the leaders.

## 34 Let's Pretend

Ask children to take turns pretending to do different kinds of jobs people have. Have the rest of the children guess what the job is. If children have trouble thinking of jobs, suggest mail carrier, waiter, nurse, bus driver, baker, and pastor.

## 35 Miniature House

Provide small boxes such as shoeboxes so children can make a miniature home. Remove the lids and turn the boxes on their sides so they look like open rooms in a doll house. Let children choose which room in the house they would like to work on: living room, kitchen, bedroom, bathroom, garage, etc. Children can create miniature furnishings to glue in the boxes with materials such as nut cups, cardboard, spools, fabric, jar lids, small gift boxes (the size that jewelry comes in), and colored paper. When the rooms are done, stack and tape the boxes together to make a miniature house.

## 36 All Week Long

The disciples found comfort in knowing that Jesus would be with them even when they were separated. Children do not always understand what happens when people go away. Talk about people the children may see only once a week such as the pastor or Sunday school teacher. What do they think these people do during the week? Tell what you do. If you know, tell them what the pastor does during the week. Help them understand what a parent who works outside the home does.

## 37 On the Go

*In advance:* Cut pictures of transportation vehicles (cars, trucks, planes, trains, bicycles, etc.) from magazines and coloring books. Also cut out pictures of familiar objects that could not be used for transportation. Place all the pictures on the table. Have the pupils point to the transportation pictures and identify them. Encourage children to tell you how those things are used.

## 38 Jesus Loves My Friends

Help each child name all the children he or she knows. Print the names on a list and talk about how Jesus loves all these children.

## 39 Pet Shop

Play "pet shop." Use cardboard boxes for cages and stuffed animals for pets. Let children take a pretend trip to purchase a pet. Name the different stuffed animals and make their sounds as you look at them. Ask: "Would this animal make a good pet?" (Tigers and teddy bears would be happier in the forest.) As you look in each cage, ask, "Who made this animal?" And after you answer this question together, say, "And everything God made was good."

## 40 It's Important!

Name things that are important to you. Help children name things that are important to them such as sleeping with a favorite stuffed animal. Then have them cut out pictures from magazines of things that are important to Jesus. Then help them realize that everyone is important to Jesus, and He cares about what is important to us.

## 41 Making Figures

Make play dough or gingerbread figures. As you work together, say that God made our arms, legs, shoulders, and heads. Have children point to the body part mentioned. Then talk about the things each body part can do. Arms reach, eyes see, and so on.

## 42 What Does It Need?

As you look at books with children, play "What Does It Need?" Point to various people and animals and ask what each needs. Perhaps children will think of food, shelter, or a hug. This game will help them start the lifelong task of putting others first.

## 43 Love Gift

Give a child a surprise gift such as a lollipop, a special sticker, small pack of crayons, or even a hug-just because you love him or her. Explain when you give the gift or hug that God does the same thing for His children. He gives us good things just because He loves us.

## 44 Watch Them Grow!

In early spring, plant marigold seeds (or any hardy annual) in small pots on a window sill. Talk about how we need to water the plant, but God puts life into the seeds and makes them grow. Let children squirt a spray bottle to keep plants moist. If possible, plant seedlings outside when danger of frost is past.

## 45 What's This For?

Play "What's This For?" pointing to different parts of our bodies. Ask what each part does to help us: feet help us walk, fingers help us color pictures, and so on. Let child try brushing his or her hair without bending an arm to show how important the elbow is to the body. Say, "Isn't it wonderful how God made our bodies to work for us?"

## 46 Pretend Sunday School

Let children take turns pretending to be the teacher telling about God at Sunday school. Provide a few props: a small table for an altar, a child's Bible, and some Sunday school cards. The "pupils" might be a few dolls. The "teacher" can lead everyone in singing and tell a Bible story.

## 47 Sorting It Out

Help children learn to categorize by giving them buttons to sort by color. If children do not know the colors, let them sort by size. Explain that God helps us learn how to do things so that we can help one another.

## 48 Making a Puzzle Person

Have a child lie on a large sheet of wrapping paper. Draw an outline of the figure. Then have the same child or another child lie on another sheet of paper. Draw an outline of the figure. Cut out the second figure, then cut it into six pieces: the two arms, the two legs, the body, and the head. Let children use this as a jigsaw puzzle, putting the pieces in the proper place on top of the first outlined figure. As children play, talk about our bodies and how wonderfully God has made them.

# 49 Water and Fish

Give each child a blue crepe paper streamer two feet long and show how to move it gently, pretending to be water. Begin slowly and gradually, then have the children move their streamers faster and faster as if the water is moving quickly.

Collect the streamers and have children put their hands together and pretend to be fish. As they "swim" around the room, quietly say:

*The fish are gently swimming, swimming, swimming.*
*The fish are gently swimming through the water.*

Change the tempo of the words to let the children move faster or slower.

# 50 Feeding Time

Put a goldfish in a bowl and fish food on a table. Have children stand next to the table and watch the fish swim around. Explain that it is important to keep hands out of the bowl or the fish might be frightened.

Put a little fish food in the bowl and watch as the fish eats. Or if you have only a few children, give each child a flake of fish food and help them individually drop the food into the bowl.

Ask: "How does a fish move? What happens when food is dropped in the water?" Explain that God made fish to live and breathe in water. Everything God made is very good.

# 51 Our Community

Begin a community mural that you may want to keep up for several weeks. Find a wall, bulletin board, room divider, or window where you can begin arranging your community.

**Buildings:** Make a house pattern children can use, or let them draw their own houses to cut from construction paper. Include houses, stores, and apartment buildings. Children who are less advanced manually may prefer to have you do the cutting, especially around doors and windows. Let them color houses on white paper, draw bricks, and so on.

**Trees and flowers:** Add construction paper trees and flowers to the mural.

**Transportation:** Have children add a variety of methods of transportation to their community mural. They may draw (or cut out) pictures of cars, trucks, buses, taxis, airplanes, trains, and bicycles. Let children tell how many of these methods of transportation they have used. How many would they like to try?

*Option:* Roll up several 6" squares of construction paper to make cylinders. Children can paste or tape a car to the top of these cylinders, which can be used as holders so the children can "drive" their cars to different places in the community.

# 52 Thank-You Banner

Use the words "Thank You, God" to make a banner for the community mural or any other bulletin board that depicts things for which we should thank God. Project the words from an overhead projector onto a large sheet of paper and trace around them, color, and cut out. Paste the words to a bright ribbon or paper banner and add balloons made from paper circles and strings. Ask children to name friends in the community for whom they are thankful.

## 53 From Farm to Store

Let children make matching farm and store pictures. Show on one sheet of paper what a food item looks like as it comes from a farm; on another paper, show that same food in a supermarket. *Examples:* Cow with pail of milk by it; plastic jug of milk. Chicken by eggs in a nest; carton of eggs. Corn in a field; corn in a can. Apple tree; bag of apples. Pumpkin patch; pumpkin pie. These pictures can be previously cut from magazines and pasted on construction paper. Connect the pictures with string or yarn. You might title this display "God Gives Us Good Things to Eat."

## 54 My Family Helps Me

Place a long piece (5 or 6 feet) of butcher paper on the wall at the children's eye level and with a crayon or marker divide the paper into five sections. In each section, print one of the following: "Mothers"; "Fathers"; "Sisters and Brothers"; "Grandparents"; "Us" (preschool children). Children can draw, or paste figures cut from magazines, in each section to represent that family member. Be sensitive to children from single parent or other non-traditional families.

After the illustrations are up, have each child tell you something each of the various people could do to help him or her do what is right. Your children will probably need help thinking of some ideas. For example, mother could tell you to eat your food, father could tell you when to go to sleep, brother or sister could tell you to stop at the curb when the light is red, grandmother could show you how to do your work, you and your friends can remind each other how to act, etc. Print these suggestions under the appropriate pictures.

## 55 Jesus Loves Everyone

Hang a piece of butcher paper low on a wall or door. At the top print: "Jesus loves everyone the same." Children may cut from magazines, catalogs, or old take home papers pictures of different people. Include young and old, people of different races and different occupations. Paste the pictures on the poster.

## 56 God Cares for His Creations

In advance, prepare a piece of shelf or butcher paper for a mural. Divide the mural into four sections. At the top of each section paste a picture of one of the following: a bird; an animal; a flower; a child. Below each picture children may paste things God gives His creations: berries, seeds, and twigs for the bird; perhaps pictures of grass and a pond for the animal; a sun and raindrops for the flower; pieces of dry cereal, cloth, and pictures of houses and families for the child.

## 57 Out on the Lake

Tape a length of butcher or shelf paper to the floor with masking tape. Draw a blue oval on the paper to represent a lake. Provide the children with crayons, scraps of construction paper, blunt-edged scissors, cotton balls, and paste or glue to make fluffy clouds, sun, boats, etc. Help children add these items to the picture, showing them how to make boats from triangles and rectangles.

Pretend that a storm starts on the lake. The wind is blowing (everybody blow). Change the picture to show that it is stormy. Help children draw big waves on the lake. Cut a dark cloud out of paper and paste it over the sun.

## 58 What Do I Do All Day?

Provide each child with a paper on which you have already drawn a sun. The sun should be in different positions on different papers at the upper left for morning, at the top middle for noon, at the upper right for afternoon, and way over to the right as if setting at night. Help children decide what time of day each picture would be and what they would be doing at that time. Older children may want to draw a picture of getting dressed in the morning. Another child may want to draw himself or herself playing outside with friends in the middle of the day. Another child may wish to portray an evening scene such as getting ready for bed.

*(Continued on next page.)*

After children have drawn pictures, post them in order from morning until night on a bulletin board or mural. Talk about how God takes care of us throughout the entire day, no matter what happens.

# 59 Fill the Ark

Cut out a large ark from brown butcher paper and tape it to a wall. Let children color or cut out and paste on pairs of animals. Decorate the animals with scraps of yarn and fake fur.

# 60 God Made the Seasons

Cover a table with a long piece of butcher paper. Mark it off into four sections: summer, fall, winter, and spring. Label the mural with the words "God Made the Seasons."

Have the children scribble color in each of the different sections. Provide them with colors related to each of the seasons. For summer provide bright colors such as yellow and bright blue; for fall provide colors such as brown, gold, and maroon; for winter provide gray and white; spring colors might be green, lavender, and pink. Adjust color choices according to the seasons in your particular area.

*Option:* Provide collage materials for the children to paste onto the mural. For example, strips of foil can be spring rain; a yellow circle can be the summer sun; torn paper or real leaves can represent fall; and cotton can be winter snow.

# 61 Building God's House

Secure a rather large cardboard carton. A stove carton would work very nicely; check with an appliance store to obtain one. Draw windows and cut out a door, so children may enter. Children can help paste on curtains made from facial tissues at the windows. Children may help you build pews of blocks. At the front of the church, make a small table of blocks and place a Bible on it. Ask children to suggest other things that might go in the church.

# 62 Telephone Line

Play "telephone" with the children. Have them sit in a circle while you whisper to the first child, "Jesus loves you." Then let that child whisper the message to the child next to him or her and so on around the circle. Have the last child say the message aloud. You might let your children think of other messages about Jesus they can send.

# 63 Playing Church

Let children act out going to church. Some children can be the congregation, the choir, and the ushers. Let children take turns being the minister.

Ask children to play other helpful things at church. They may act out ways they can help, such as sweeping the floors, setting up chairs, and so on.

# 64 Christmas All Year

When you take down your Christmas tree, keep one ornament in your room. Choose one which will remind children of the Christmas message that Jesus is the promised Savior: a star, an angel, or a tiny Nativity scene. Hang the ornament in a place where the children will see it often and remember that God sent Jesus to be our Savior at Christmas and all year long.

# 65 When I'm Scared

Have older children get together in pairs or small groups to act out some scary situations. (Suggestions: thunderstorm; barking dog; "monsters under the bed"; the dark; etc.) After each skit, let volunteers name and then act out ways to let God help. (They can pray; talk to their families so they can help; sing a song about God; and so on.)

# 66 We Can Worship

Talk about the various skills that God has given each child and how each child can use his or her skills to share in God's work. Then help children plan a mini worship service so that youngsters can use their skills. Pick a theme for the service ahead of time so all of the children's efforts will emphasize the chosen theme. Let children choose what they'd like to do:

• Play rhythm instruments and/or sing a simple worship song.

• Work on a group prayer or action rhyme to recite together.

• Illustrate a favorite Bible story by drawing pictures, painting a mural, or making a sculpture.

• Act out the Bible story.

• Set up and arrange items such as chairs and art displays.

If the group is small, just one child might do each job, or the jobs could overlap. Just be certain that each child is given the opportunity to participate actively and to contribute to the group effort.

# 67 This Is the Way We

Help children think of ways they might help a sick friend. Then let children pretend to do these things. For example, if someone suggests, "Take flowers," the following steps may be acted out: walking to the garden; picking the flowers; carrying them carefully to the sick friend's house; ringing the doorbell; greeting the friend's mother at the door; presenting the flowers to the mother to give to the friend; saying good-bye; skipping home.

# 68 Friends Help Each Other

God showed Elisha how to be a good friend to a woman and her sons. Pray with children that God will help all of you show friendship. Then help children plan friendly gestures you can do together for someone who needs help.

• Prepare food and deliver it to someone who is sick.

• Take an elderly person grocery shopping.

• Transport a neighbor child to Sunday school.

• Help rake a neighbor's lawn.

# 69 A Friend Loves

Do you know someone who is sick, shut-in, or just lonely? Sending cards to friends and involving children in mailing them will be meaningful. Encourage children to draw a special picture to include. Imagine the smile on someone's face when a card arrives saying, "A friend always loves you."

## 70 Weather-Wise

What weather is it today? Thank God for the weather-no matter what it is during prayer time. Avoid labeling weather as "nice" or "bad." Instead, talk about how all kinds of weather help us and the animals and plants.

Show pictures of types of things such as boots, sunglasses, umbrellas, swimsuits, and wool scarves, that are needed for different weather conditions. Have children guess the type of weather during which each is used.

## 71 Sunlight Delight

Make a point to look with your child for sunshine, shadows, and clouds each day. We often take daylight for granted, especially in a city where the sky maybe crowded out by buildings. Tell children that God created the sun that shines as they work and play. Take a walk and point out things that people can do during the day. You may see someone mowing the grass, watering flowers, or riding a bicycle. Note that the bright sun gives us light even when it is cloudy.

## 72 Signs of the Seasons

Weather permitting, take a nature walk with children to see signs of the season, whichever it may be. If you take your walk during spring, point out to them the buds on trees, birds returning, warmer weather, and crocus blooming. Sing a song about that season while you walk.

## 73 Rain, Rain, It's Okay

When it rains, remind children of the story of Noah and the ark. Forty days was a long rain! If the rain is not too hard, dress appropriately and take a walk outside. Thank God for the beautiful trees, animals, grass, and flowers that are getting a bath and a drink. Be ready to look for rainbows when the sun shines during a summer shower. Talk about how we obey God when we thank Him as Noah did.

## 74 Sharing God's Love

Share God's love. This activity can be done in the classroom or at home. Make mini hearts from red scrap paper. Hide a few around the room, under things or in pockets. Tell the finder of each heart, "I love you and so does God."

Share love and cheer others. Draw simple hearts on postcards and let children color them. Add a message of God's love and send cards to neighbors and your pastor.

## 75 Showing Love

Have children pretend that their dolls have done something wrong, such as pushing or saying something mean. Help children to act out a way that their dolls could do what is right. Encourage the children to hug their dolls and show them love, both when they have done wrong and when they have done what is right.

## 76 Sharing Cookies

Bake a favorite sugar cookie recipe with the children. Write special messages on little slips of paper, roll them up, then shape some dough around each little roll of paper and bake. Be sure to explain the messages to the children since they can't read. Have them help you think of people to whom they can give the cookies: church neighbors, shut-ins, a friend who's been sick. Messages can fit various holidays:

**Christmas:** "Hallelujah! Jesus is born,"
**Valentine:** "Jesus loves you; I do, too."
**Thanksgiving:** "We thank God for you."

## Just for Fun Activities

### 77 Playing Animals

Here are some ways children will enjoy pretending to be animals:

- Suggest that some children pretend to be pets, such as cats and dogs. Other children can take care of them by "feeding" them and taking them for a walk.

- Pretend to have a zoo. Make block enclosures and let some children be the animals in the zoo. Others may be the zoo keepers and take care of the animals.

- Children might enjoy having a parade in which each pretends to be a certain animal. Make animal noises as you walk around the room.

### 78 Penny Walk

On a nice day, go for a penny walk. Walk to the corner and flip a penny. Heads you go one way, tails you go another way. Where will you end up?

### 79 Noise Makers

For each child, place a few beans or buttons in a small plastic container or ice cream carton (pint size). Tape the lid securely to the carton. Children will delight in shaking this rhythm instrument and marching in time with music. Let the children suggest happy songs to sing while they shake their instruments.

### 80 "Holes" to Crawl Through

To help get out the wiggles, let children crawl through "holes," These holes could be under tables or adult-size chairs; through large boxes; or the holes could be created when you stand with your legs apart or lean against the wall.

### 81 Mother, May I?

Play the traditional game, "Mother, May I?" Explain to children that you are the leader, and in this game the leader is called "Mother." Place children side by side in a line. Stand about three yards in front of them and, speaking to one child at a time by name, give an order: take three little steps, or two giant steps, or two big hops, and so on. Vary your orders, but be sure the children are able to do what you are asking. Some children have trouble jumping, skipping, or hopping on one foot.

Instruct children that the rules of the game say that they must remember to ask, "Mother, may I?" before they do what was commanded. Answer the child by saying, "Yes, you may!" If a child forgets to ask permission first, he or she loses a turn.

Be sure to give each child several opportunities to move forward. The winner is the first child to reach the area where you are standing.

### 82 Sandals

Draw a pattern around the child's stocking feet on poster board or cardboard. Make the pattern a little larger than the child's feet. Lace yarn or strips of fabric through holes at the toes and the heels. Tie the yarn or fabric at the ankle and over the toes.

### 83 Free-Form Collage

Have ready a large piece of shelf or butcher paper and a variety of collage materials such as: scraps of fabric; tissue paper; yarn; macaroni; or buttons. Explain that a collage is a picture made from all different kinds of materials. Give each child all of one type of material. If you do not have enough variety of materials, give two or three children all the yarn and another pair all the buttons, etc.

Let children glue their items onto the shelf paper in any way they wish. As they work, talk to them about working together.

## 84 Bean Bag Toss

Make a bean bag toss game. Bean bags can be made of two 6" squares of fabric filled with rice or beans and stitched securely together.

To make a target, tape four shoe boxes together: (1) tape two boxes side by side; (2) tape a third box across the top ends of the first two boxes; (3) tape the fourth box across the bottom ends.

Number the boxes 1 through 4. The box at the bottom should be number 1, the two boxes in the middle should be 2 and 3. and the box at the top should be 4.

Children can take turns throwing bean bags, trying to toss the bags into the number 4 section. Talk about how much fun it is to play together as well as to work together.

## 85 House Puzzle

Give each child the following construction paper shapes: 4" square, two 1" squares, a 1" x 3" rectangle, and a triangle, measuring 5" across the bottom and 3 1/2" on either side. Children will also need an 8 1/2" x 11" piece of construction paper. Have them paste or glue the shapes on the construction paper to make a house. Rather than making a sample for the children to copy, you might help them think through what shapes would go where to make a house.

## 86 Airplane on a String

Cut a simple airplane shape from a piece of cardboard or heavy paper. Punch a hole in the top of the plane. Tie one end of a 10-foot piece of string to a chair or another piece of furniture. Thread the loose end of the string through a hole in the plane. Push the plane all the way back to the chair. Stretch the line of string out straight and give the end to a child to hold.

Let each child take a turn jiggling the string carefully to get the plane to move toward him or her.

Use these ideas with your own family or send them home in notes as family time ideas for the children in your class.

## 87 Be Kind Suggestion Box

Keep a suggestion box for "Be Kind to Others" ideas near your dinner table or wherever your family has devotions. Jot down ideas for kind things that can be done for others and put them into the box. Once a week, let your child pick one suggestion from the box to do. Ideas might include calling a new neighbor, giving a family member a warm hug, or telling someone he or she looks nice.

## 88 God Made Food

When you shop with your children, point out the many different kinds of fruits and vegetables in the store. If you are not in a rush, talk about where these foods came from. For example, apples grow on apple trees and God made trees.

Continue this conversation as your child helps you put away groceries or fix supper. Discuss how carrots, potatoes, and other fruits and vegetables grew from tiny seeds in the ground. Alter each item is named, you and your child can say together, "And everything God made was good."

## 89 Learning to Share

Help your child learn to share by asking him or her to choose one or two books or toys in good condition to give to a child who doesn't have many. Or go shopping together and allow your child to buy two inexpensive toys or games; on the way home help your child place one in a drop box for a local charity.

## 90 Preparing for Church

Involve your child in preparations for church. Cleaning shoes, clearing out the car, laying out offering-all these chores can be done with the happy anticipation that "tomorrow is the day we worship God with our church family."

## 91 The Bible at Home

Let your child see that daily Bible reading is part of your family routine even though he or she cannot yet understand long Scripture passages. Try to schedule a time, perhaps before bedtime, when you can read simple Bible stories to your child and talk about what they mean.

## 92 Giving to God

Help your child be a part of the giving experience by providing a container where your child can put coins for a Sunday school offering: a piggy bank, a pretty jar with a lid, almost anything will do. It might be fun to decorate a shoe box to use for offerings. Cut slots in the lid and add labels showing different ways your offerings are used.

## 93 I Can Help!

Assign your child specific chores to help at home. Keep a colorful chart with each day's chores checked off (brush teeth, put away toys, dust table) to encourage obedience in a fun way. Be sure to mention that we show love to God when we obey.

## 94 Our Family Rules

Draw simple pictures on paper listing your important family rules: "Don't hit brother"; "Wash hands before meals"; "Say please and thank you"; and so forth. Put the picture chart on the refrigerator to remind your child what he or she should do to be happy and make God happy.

## 95 Where Food Comes From

At a mealtime, name the different foods on the table that God has provided. Don't go into detail about where meat comes from. However, do talk about the sources of fruits, vegetables, bread, milk, and so on. As you name each food, thank God for it.

## 96 Family Christmas Program

Your whole family might want to have a Christmas program at home using robes and towels for costumes. You can take photographs and mount them in a notebook with the Christmas story. Then read it together during the holiday season.

## 97 Caring for Pets

Involve children in caring for family pets: feeding, watering, changing cage or litter, brushing, etc. Show children how to be gentle with animals and not startle them with loud noises or movements. Talk with children about the special way God made the cat's whiskers or soft hair. Tell children that God is pleased when we care for and enjoy the animals He has made.

## 98 Welcome to My House

Invite your pastor or child's Sunday school teacher for dessert. Encourage your child to participate in the preparations and in the conversation. Your child will have a new appreciation of the pastor or teacher as a real person.

## 99 Pretend Restaurant

At lunch time, let children fix up a restaurant table and pretend they are being served or are serving in a restaurant. Take orders; bring the "special of the day" (soup, crackers, sandwich, and juice could be served). Remember good manners. Leave a tip!

## 100 Prayer Calendar

On a large calendar, write down the name of at least one person per day to remember with a special prayer. Keep it simple so that your child can understand and be a part of prayer time. During family devotional time or at your child's bedtime, talk about why you need to pray for that person. Then encourage your child to mention the person's name in prayer.

# 100 More Activities for Ages 3-5

## Bible Story Activities

### 1 God Separates the Water

Demonstrate God separating the water from the land in this way. Fill a large dishpan 1/4 full of sand and add a few large rocks. Add water until sand and rocks are covered. Push the sand to one side with one hand and the "land" and "mountains" will appear.

### 2 God Cares for Birds

Gather around a parakeet, canary, or other pet bird in a cage. Encourage the children to talk in soft voices so as not to frighten it. If the bird is tame, bring it out on your finger; otherwise just watch it in its cage.

Help the children enjoy the bird by asking some of the following questions:

What colors are the bird's feathers?

How did the bird get dressed this morning?

What kind of sound does the bird make?

What does it eat?

### 3 Find the Lost Sheep

After telling the Bible story of Jesus and the lost sheep, talk about what a difficult task it was to find a little lost sheep in the night with no flashlight. Explain that the shepherd would have had to use his ears to listen carefully for the sound of the sheep. Then let children play a game of blind tag called "Find the Lost Sheep." The "lost sheep" will stand or hide somewhere in the room and say a soft "baa" every few seconds. The rest of the children must keep their eyes closed and search for the sheep using only their hands and their ears. The child who finds the sheep gets to be the "lost sheep" in the next round.

### 4 Hungry Lambs

In this game one child is chosen as a shepherd. The, shepherd's job is to tag the hungry lambs who are "baaing." This quiets the sheep. After each hungry lamb is tagged, he or she must count to ten before "baaing" again. See if the shepherd can get everyone quiet at once.

### 5 Wolf!

Choose one child to be a shepherd and another to be a wolf. All the rest play sheep. During play, the wolves make the sound of "grrrr" and the sheep "baaa." Sheep try to stay away from wolves, but if tagged by a wolf, that "sheep" becomes a wolf. All wolves try to tag sheep without being tagged by the shepherd. If the shepherd tags a wolf, the wolf becomes a sheep again. Play for a minute at a time. Count to see how many sheep are left. Play several times with different starting characters. Stay within a designated area.

### 6 What's It Like?

This activity will be especially meaningful if done after either the story of blind Bartimaeus or the ten lepers. Children may never have thought about what it feels like to miss out on things because of a physical disability. This activity will give children the opportunity to find out what it's like to be blind, or to be without the use of a leg.

Let volunteers take turns being blindfolded. Have each volunteer feel the face of two or three children and try to guess who they are. Use the blindfold to tie a volunteer's leg in a bent position. Have the volunteers try to walk, pushing a small chair in front of them for balance. Talk about how Jesus showed His love for people with special needs by taking time to notice their problems and heal them.

## 7 Fishing for Good News

Cover a large box with a blue sheet or blanket. Children cast string with a bent paper clip hook into the "water." Sit behind the box, attaching a paper fish to the lines thrown in. On the fish should be written a Bible verse.

## 8 Tea Party

After telling the story of Jesus at the home of Simon the Pharisee, let children give a "tea party" of their own. Food can be "pretend," or you might choose to have lemonade and graham crackers for the children to serve. Choose one child to be the host, one to be the honored guest, and have the rest take the parts of the other guests. Let children dress up in old adult clothing from a dress-up trunk. Encourage everyone to be very polite and friendly at their tea party!

## 9 Riding the Donkey

Children line up as for "London Bridge." They pass through the "gate to Jerusalem" as they sing these words to the tune.

**Riding to Jerusalem
Through the gate, through the gate.
Riding to Jerusalem
On a donkey!**

When children are "caught," give each one a palm branch to wave as the game continues.

## 10 My Own Garden

Give each child a piece of brown paper or section of brown paper bag. On it, they may paste pictures cut from catalogs or magazines of things they would like to grow in a garden. Remind children that God made all the plants and He wants us to take care of them.

## 11 Alive and Not Alive

With masking tape, make two large circles on the floor. Label one circle "Alive" and the second "Not Alive." Collect items that are alive (plants, small animals, and pictures of people) and not alive (chairs, toy trucks, and rocks). Talk to the children about living things: they breathe, grow, need food and oxygen. Talk about non-living things and compare them to living things. Put each item you have collected in the appropriate circle on the floor. Remove the items from the circles and let children categorize them. Remind children that God gives us life. He makes things grow.

## 12 Feel, Touch, and Smell

For "feel" bring an electric box fan. Turn it on and let the children feel the air blowing on them. Emphasize that we know the air is blowing even though we cannot see it.

For "touch" put several objects (such as a small rock, a crayon, a spoon, and a glove) in a small cloth bag. Have children feel the object in the bag and guess what it is. Emphasize that we know the object is there even though we do not see it.

For "smell" use foods, flowers, and other aromatic substances. Have one or two children blindfolded and guess what the objects are simply by smelling them. Let children take turns using the blindfolds. Emphasize that the objects are there even though we don't see them.

## 13 Traffic signs

Show the children pictures of flash cards of different traffic signs. Have the children try to guess what the signs tell people to do. Discuss what the signs mean. Point out that road signs are rules that tell us what to do to be safe.

## 14 Banking Fun

Children think it's great fun to handle money, because it's usually "off-limits" to them. Bring in several old purses, wallets, and play money. If you have a box of coins, let the children play with those. Or, let them look at a collection of foreign money. Talk about the similarities and differences of the money of different countries.

Let the children play bank, and decide what part of their money they will save, what they will spend, and what they will give to help others. Explain at the beginning of the activity that you're not really giving them money-it's just for play, and you will collect it all at the end. Praise God for giving us the money we need to live, plus enough to share with others.

## 15 Little Seeds Grow

Provide moistened potting soil and disposable planting containers such as margarine tubs. Let the children spoon soil into the planters and push seeds down in the dirt. Beans sprout well and quickly. Sunflowers are also successful and when transplanted grow taller than the children. Growing plants is a very special way of experiencing God's miracles of growth.

## 16 Feed the Birds

Give each child a piece of bread. Help them to remove the crusts and set aside. Show the children how to mold the bread into a ball. Help the children tie a length of string or yarn around the ball of bread. Take the bread outside and tie onto a low tree or bush branches. Scatter the bread crusts on the ground. Tell children that the birds will also use the string or yarn in building nests.

## 17 Being the Teacher

Most children really enjoy an opportunity to take center stage. Allow them to take turns being the teacher. Talk about how Jesus went around teaching people, and that teaching about God's love is very important work. Give children a choice about what to teach. It may be a Bible verse, a mini sermon or a song. A few articles of old adult clothing will add to the fun of the activity.

## 18 Footprints

As you visit the zoo, take along some paper to sketch on. Look for as many different kinds of animal foot-prints as you can find. Draw a simple copy of each and let your child help to label them. Talk about how God created animals with certain kinds of feet to do special things, like the duck's webbed ones which help in swimming.

## 19 Who Are You?

Have the children sit in a circle. Talk briefly with them about our identity with families. Ask the question, "Who are you?" The children will answer by giving their name. You may want to go around the circle several times. Each time have the children answer a different way (by gender, "I'm a girl," or by age, "I'm four years old.")

## 20 Everything God Made Was Good

Staple three sheets of white paper between two sheets of construction paper. On the front write "Everything God Made Was Good." Inside, the children may paste pictures cut from magazines of different things God made. How wonderful to have a book of God's creation to read over and over again.

## 21 Surprise Bag of Teaching Things

Fill a paper bag with items such as a mixing spoon, story book, crayon, ball, and Bible. As items are pulled from the bag, have children identify them and how they are used by adults to teach children things.

## 22 Who Goes to Church?

Glue pictures of people and objects around the edges of several paper plates. Children can attach clothes pins to the pictures of people that can worship God in church.

## 23 All Kinds of Houses

Give each child an 8 1/2" x 11" paper and a choice of various paper shapes including big and small squares, triangles, and rectangles. Let them each construct a house by laying out the shapes and pasting them down.

## 24 Taking Care of Others

While looking at books and pictures, help children suggest ways they can help care for plants and animals. What are some things they can do when they're older? Can they start now caring for things in a small way?

## 25 Love Chain

This activity will give children a graphic representation of the people in the church who love them. Give each child a strip of paper 4" x 1/2". Help them think of someone in the church who loves them. Write the name of that person on the paper strip of the first child and form into a ring. Continue in this manner, interlocking rings to form a chain. Children can keep adding links as long as there are people to name. A pictorial directory will be helpful. How long is the love chain for your class?

## 26 Our Families

Put out clay or play dough. As children cut out cookie-cutter people, arrange them in family groups representing the children's families. This will help you get to know the families of each child and give the children another opportunity to thank God for their families.

## 27 Protection Inspection

In this activity children will make an "inspection glass" (to look like a magnifying glass) by gluing two 4" construction paper circles with the centers cut out to a craft stick. You might want to glue clear kitchen wrap in the "glass" to make it look authentic. Children can use these to look for signs that parents and adults care for them, or to see signs of God's work in our world.

## 28 I'm Looking for a Friend

Give one child a beanbag. That child walks around the circle while you sing these words to the tune *Farmer in the Dell.*

**I'm looking for a friend.**
**I'm looking for a friend.**
**Drop the beanbag, 1, 2, 3.**
**I'm looking for a friend.**

The child drops the beanbag behind a friend and takes that child's place in the circle so there is a new person walking with the beanbag.

## 29 Night and Day

Have the children sit in a circle. Show two pieces of paper, one white and one black. Explain that white makes us think of day, which is light, while black makes us think of night which is dark. Place both sheets in the middle of the circle.

Your children can take turns tossing a beanbag. If it lands on black, they state something about the night; if it lands on white, they say something about day.

## 30 Whatever Is It?

Draw things in the air with your finger and have children guess what they are. You may need to give the children clues. Here are some examples:

Draw a large, round sun with sunbeams.
Clue: It shines in the sky and keeps us warm.
Draw a tree.
Clue: It has leaves and fruit grows on it sometimes.

## 31 Name Game

Ask the children to sit in a circle. Have the first child say his or her name. Have the second child repeat the first child's name and say his or her own name and so on around the circle. You or your helper should be the last one to say all the names. And you or your helper might need to help the children in repeating the names of the others.

## 32 Who Is My Friend?

Have the children sit in a circle. The leader should start the game by asking, "Can you guess who my friend is?" One clue should be given such as, "My friend is wearing a green dress." Continue giving clues until the children have guessed who the person is (be sure the friend you are describing is in the circle). The child that guessed the identity of the friend should take a turn or go around the circle giving each child a turn to describe someone else.

## 33 Friend Loves

Have children sit in a circle on the floor. The leader should walk around the circle, tapping each child on the head while repeating, "A friend loves at all times." After a few taps say, "A friend loves when. . ." The child whose head is tapped this last time should offer an example of when a friend loves (e.g., when a friend shares a toy, when a child prays for a friend, when a child lets a friend go first at the water fountain). This child should then be the "leader." Be sure each child gets a turn to be "leader."

## 34 Mother/Father Says

Play a variation of "Simon Says" using the words "Mother (or Father) says . . ." If the command is, "Sweep the floor," children should stay still. If the command is, "Mother says sweep the floor," children should do the action. Children must listen closely.

## 33 Join the Circle

In this activity, the leader will choose children from the group, two at a time, to join in a circle. Each time the leader chooses new children, the leader will say, "God loves Cindy" or "God loves Matthew," using the name of each child. Then they will all join hands and walk in a circle while singing the following song to the tune of *God Is So Good*.

God loves us all.
God loves us all.
God loves us all. He loves you and me!

Keep adding children, two at a time, and singing the song each time until the whole group is holding hands and walking in a circle.

## 36 Good Teachers

Play a game of "musical chairs" where everyone is a winner. Set chairs in a row with enough chairs for everyone to be seated. Play music on the cassette tape recorder or record player. When the music stops children are seated, and you may choose one child to name someone who can tell him or her about Jesus. Give the children who name someone (even with help) a sticker of Jesus to wear.

## 37 Name the Helper

In this game, children will act out various types of jobs that helpers do. (Pretending to preach like a pastor, to spray a building like a fire fighter, etc.) The rest of the class tries to guess the helper being acted out. The children may choose a helper or take a suggestion from the leader.

## 38 Guess Who?

Divide children into two groups. Hold up a sheet between them. Group one will be guessers, group two will choose one person at a time to stick his or her foot under the sheet so the guessers can see it. Can the guessers guess who? Give each child in group two a turn to stick a foot under the sheet and be guessed, then switch sides.

## 39 Obey the Rules

To play this game you will need a piece of red paper and a piece of green paper. Children stand behind a line and the leader says, "Rules are important to obey. When I hold up the green paper, all children may take a step forward. When I hold up the red, all children stand still." Since the children are moving at the same speed they should all cross the finish line at the same time and be winners.

## 40 Who Am I?

Whisper the name of a bird, animal, or plant to a child. The child can say, "Who Am I?" then act out his or her bird, animal, or plant. Other children can guess.

If a child has trouble knowing what to do, here are a few suggestions: *Bird*—pecking out of a shell, flapping wings, or pecking seeds from ground. *Flower*—crouch down, then slowly stand up with hands together overhead; open hands to represent flower. *Squirrel*—hold nut in hands and nibble; scurry around.

## 41 Musical Disciples

One child stands in the center of the circle with eyes closed. Children march around the circle until the music stops. Child in the center raises arm and points to one child who gets to be the next one in the circle. Remind children that no one gets to be chosen all the time, but each of them is special to Jesus.

## 42 Divided Picture of Kind Deeds

Find five or six pictures of people doing kind things. Magazines and old Sunday school papers are good sources for this. Mount pictures on different colored construction paper, then cut mounted pictures in half. Hide the divided pictures around the room and hunt for them. Match the pieces and name the helper.

## 43 How Do I Know?

This guessing game is played by describing some-thing and asking children to guess what you're describing. For example, you might say, "I am thinking of something that's juicy, sweet, red, round, and good to eat. What is it?" (The answer is apple.) When someone guesses the right answer, allow them to whisper to you, the next item to be described.

## 44 Toss and Grow

Use a baby blanket and a soft ball. Children can hold corners and edges of the blanket. One child tosses the ball into the center of the blanket and all pull on the blanket to make it bounce. As you do this they can say "Thank You, God, that (child's name) is growing up." When the ball bounces off the blanket, another child may toss it in and be the subject of the refrain.

## 45 Let's Visit a Friend

Children can play a simple game about going to see a friend. As you go around the circle, each one says, "When I go to see my friend, I like to take_____ (insert something friends would enjoy together). If children really like this game, they could go around again, and add something new to take on their visit, say-ing both things the second time around.

## 46 God Is with Me

The leader has cards with pictures of various places on them such as a doctor's office, school building, house, etc. Holding cards down so she/he can't see the pictures, the leader invites a child to draw one card. All of the children can see the card, but not the leader. The leader then has to guess which pic-ture is on the card. When the correct guess is made the leader says,"God is with us when we're at (name the place pictured on the card)."

## 47 Building a Prayer Place

Provide very large blocks or cardboard boxes and let the children build an enclosure several levels high. Describe it as a special place to pray. Encourage them to pray a short prayer in their enclosure. Also stress that Jesus is with us wherever we are, but sometimes people like to have special places to pray. Ask them if there is a special place at their house where they would like to pray.

## 48 Helping Pennies

Trace around pennies on a large chart. When children bring pennies they can tape them to the chart. When the chart is filled the class can use the money to help others.

## 49 Frosting Cookies

Provide the children with sugar cookies or graham crackers to spread with canned icing. Let them each make two treats, one to eat and one to share.

## 50 Going to Church

Use dress-up clothes such as aprons, ties, belts, and coats to portray adults. (Avoid shoes and hats for health reasons.) Dress baby dolls and take them to church. The children will thank God for adults who take them to church.

## 51 My Friends

Children should sit in a circle. The children can practice introducing each other. The leader should start by saying "Hi, my name is [insert name] and this is my friend [child on the right]." The child introduced would then do the same introducing the child on his or her right. Continue in this manner until all the children in the circle have had a turn.

## 52 Friends Share

Encourage children to act out different situations when sharing is difficult. For example, two friends want to play with a toy. What can they do to resolve conflict in a happy way? Other situations: When one friend has a new birthday present; when two friends want to paint but there is only one brush; when two friends are playing a game and a third child comes along. Talk about how they feel when they share and how they feel when they don't share.

## 53 I Want to Share

Children should sit on the floor in a circle, legs extended and feet touching the foot of the person on the right and the left. The leader says, "I want to share this ball with (child's name)," and roll the ball to that child. That child then chooses another friend and says, "I want to share this ball with (second child's name)," and rolls the ball. The leader may suggest names so that every child gets one or more turns to share.

**Alternative:** Children may sit on chairs. The leader holds a toy enjoyed by both girls and boys (ball, stuffed animal, etc.) and says, "I want to share this toy with (child's name)," then gets up and walks over to chosen child and gives the toy. That child then chooses another child to receive the toy, and so on.

## 54 Hide-a-Treat

This fun activity will help children see the importance of sharing. Before the session begins, hide several wrapped candies around the room. Make sure there is one piece per child. At an appropriate time in your discussion about sharing, tell the children that you have brought a treat to share with all of them, but they're going to have to find it. Give instructions that no one should eat the treat, just find one and sit back down.

Discuss with the children that you shared a treat with them and they shared, too, by finding just one candy so that everyone could enjoy a treat.

## 55 Wash 'n Scrub

Children like to play at cleaning up, and it's an important part of the way they learn. Things like squirt bottles, paper towels, and dishpans full of suds are a fascinating invitation to fun. So let them go at it!

You may wish to make simple cleaning smocks from large paper grocery bags to protect clothes from splashes. Cut a seam up the back, and nice, big comfortable holes for neck and arms. You will need a large garbage bag to hold the used paper towels and "smocks." Be sure to praise the children for the excellent job they did!

## 56 Chenille Wire People

Bend the middle of a long chenille wire into a small round loop for the head. Straighten the two ends and use them as legs. Wrap a shorter wire around the middle of the figure for arms. Use these figures for acting out family situations, ways of praise and worship, or ways of apologizing with hugs or prayers.

## 57 People of God

Give each child a paper plate. After they draw pictures of their faces on them, add yarn hair. On mural paper, draw stick figures and attach the paper plate heads. God loves all of them!

## 58 God Loves You!

After you have experienced God's love together, share it! Children can trace and cut out red paper hearts. On each write, "God loves you!" Give each child two or three to give to family and friends during the week. If there are extras, mail some to a shut-in or any children absent from this activity.

## 59 Kind Friends

Give each child a partner. Let them explore the room or outside looking for pennies or hidden notes. The notes can have a Bible verse on it about friends.

## 60 Helpers

Children sometimes feel they can't help because painting the house or mowing the lawn are jobs that are too big. Comment on instances you see of children helping others such as picking up crayons, throwing away papers, or handing out drinks. Tell children you are grateful to God that they can be such good helpers. Have children suggest other ways they can be helpers in the classroom.

## 61 Church Friends

Building a church with blocks will require cooperation and help. After the church is built, each child can make a figure from chenille wires to represent someone going to church. You may wish to have them make pews and other church furniture out of small boxes. The children can use the church they built to worship God.

## 62 Babies Welcome

Let the children set up a nursery. Use shoe boxes for beds with scrap material for blankets. Child-sized chairs and cloth scraps for diapers plus assorted feeding utensils will provide a place to talk about family care and love.

## 63 Who Does Jesus Love?

On mural paper, write the words "Who does Jesus love?" Provide children with people pictures cut from magazines and catalogs. If possible you may use an instant camera to add the children's pictures to the mural, too. After the picture is complete, answer the question: Everyone!

## 64 Reasons for Seasons

Divide a paper into four sections. In each, draw a simple frame house. Children will add various objects to show different seasons. You might try cotton balls for snow or clouds, strips of tin foil for rain, torn green tissue paper for grass, and stickers of birds and flowers. God made each season so plants and animals can live and grow.

## 65 Healthful Foods Collage

Provide a large sheet of butcher paper and an assortment of old magazines for the children. Let them choose pictures of nutritious foods from magazines. Help them paste these to butcher paper. Talk about how Jesus wants us to be healthy and that includes being smart about what we eat.

## 66 Class Rules Mural

Most children don't mind a few rules, especially if they have some say in setting them! Let your children help establish a few rules for your worship time. Discuss what's most important to keep your time together fun and enjoyable for everyone. Explain that the rules need to be clear and simple, and that you don't want too many. Let children make suggestions as you jot them down. Write your final list of three to five rules on a long sheet of shelf paper. Let the children draw pictures to illustrate each rule.

## 67 Who Can Help?

Divide mural paper into sections for each child. Children can paste pictures in their section that show people helping others. At the top write "Who can help?" Label each section with the name of the child who added the pictures.

## 68 God Loves Us All!

Trace the hands and feet of each child onto colored paper. Cut them out and paste on mural paper with the name of each child by the appropriate cut outs. Isn't it wonderful that even though we are all different we can work together to make something as special as this mural?

## 69 Praise Him

Let children choose from magazine and catalog pictures things they would like to paste onto a mural. Title the display, "Reasons to Thank Jesus." It is important that even young children realize the source of all good things is Jesus and His love.

## Family Activities

## 70 Prayer Sticks

Glue pictures of individual family members and friends to craft sticks. Store them in an envelope or small jar. At family prayer time, have your child pull out a stick and pray for the person whose picture is on it.

## 71 God Made Colors

Help your child appreciate all of the colors God made by having special color days around the house. For example, on "Red Day" help your child dress in red clothes. Serve something red at each meal (strawberry jam, spaghetti, or apples). If you have time to go for a walk, try to find all the red things you can.

## 72 Building a Prayer

Help your child build a prayer by asking what he or she wants to pray about. You can suggest the child include different kinds of things: things to be thankful for, things to ask God for, expressions of praise or love for God, etc. To begin the prayer, mention a thanksgiving and have the child pray a sentence prayer; mention a request and have the child pray another simple sentence, etc.

## 73 Clean As All Outdoors

Go outside and do activities that show care for the environment. Picking up garbage, raking leaves, sweeping steps can all be done with child-sized tools. Children can even weed the garden with some direction.

## 74 Prayer Chain

Make a group or family prayer chain. Use strips of construction paper about 1" x 8". Use one color for prayer requests, another for thanksgivings, and a third for answered prayers. Form each strip into a circle and tape or staple the ends together after slipping it through the last "chain."

## Just for Fun Activities

### 75 Picture Pose

Look at picture books of families helping one another. Encourage the children to "picture pose" some of the pictures. That means they get into the same positions as the people in the picture. They can also act out what they think happens next.

### 76 Finger Flowers

Provide circle stickers and several ink pads. Place a sticker on paper for the center of the flower. Children press their fingers onto the pad and then onto the paper around the sticker to form the petals of the flower. Children will praise God for the wonders of spring.

### 77 Nature Squish Bags

To let children handle some of the things God made put sand, loose dirt, or water in freezer bags that snap closed. (You may want to double bag the items and seal them with masking tape to avoid spills.) Then have children put their hands behind their backs and instruct them not to look at the bags you will give them. See if they can figure out what's in the bag without looking.

### 78 Bubble Prints

Make bubble print cards by mixing 1/4 cup water, 20 drops of liquid food coloring, and 2 tablespoons of liquid detergent in a large bowl. Make a mound of bubbles using an eggbeater. Then lay a piece of paper over the bubbles, causing them to adhere to the paper. Paper will soon be covered with the prints of popped bubbles. Use the paper to make cards.

### 79 Family Puppets

Give each child a craft stick to represent each member of the family.

Children can add features with markers, then glue on scraps of material for clothing and yarn for hair.

### 80 Building a Wall

Use shoe boxes to make building blocks that don't make much noise. Tape the boxes shut. Children can stack them to make buildings.

### 81 Musical Instruments

Children can make the following simple instruments:

Kazoo—Fold wax paper over the teeth of a pocket comb. Hold in place with rubber bands on each end. Hum on the comb to make kazoo sounds.

Bells—String several small bells on a piece of ribbon or string about 6" long. Tie and shake.

### 82 Messy Friends

Children will each choose a partner. Each pair will work on one picture with finger paint. This may be messy so make sure the area and children's clothing are protected. Painting with a friend is twice the fun!

### 83 More Than Blocks

Some small toys added to the block area will expand imaginations and make learning fun. Include small figures of people, cars and other transportation, and street signs cut from paper and taped to a craft stick in a mound of clay. Use the additional figures to talk about obeying, sharing, and cooperating.

## 84 Going on a Picnic

No matter how miserable the weather is outside, you can pretend to go on a picnic. Think of what you would pack and then carry the picnic basket and blanket around the room until you find a good place. Give thanks before serving a small snack.

## 85 Signs to Obey

Help children glue red, yellow, and green circles on a rectangle of black paper to make a traffic signal. Then teach them to point to the colors as you say this rhyme.

Stop and sing a song of joy. Wait for your friends and share your toys. Go tell everyone you know our Lord Jesus loves you so!

## 86 Quiet Pets

Collect smooth stones for the bodies of animals. Glue on paper legs, a head, and a tail or form these features from chenille wires. Add wiggle eyes and use tempera paint to add markings. How many different animals are there in your zoo? God made them all!

## 87 Telephone

Tie loops in the ends of a piece of string. Place the loops over the thumbs of two children. They can pretend to talk to each other by holding up the thumb for an earpiece and little finger for a mouth-piece. Make the string short enough that it does not tangle around others. What good news can they share on the phone?

## 88 Find a Friend's Name

In advance, print a pair of children's names on two slips of paper. Hide the slips of paper in fairly obvious places in the room. Tell the children to search for the slip with their own name, pick it up, and sit down to wait until everyone has found their name. Help children "read" their friend's name on the slips of paper. Let the pairs of friends go to an activity center together.

## 89 Rub-a-Dub-Dub

Explore the texture of different items by doing "rubbings." Place a sheet of paper over the item and rub over the area with a crayon or soft pencil. Notice the patterns that appear!

**Nature rubbings:** Use flat items, such as leaves, pressed flowers, and tree bark.

**Building materials:** Do rubbings of brick, wood, and cement.

**Household items:** Try book covers with embossed or raised print, a cheese grater, and a lace doily.

## 90 Spring Walk

On a paper, draw simple line drawings of spring things such as flowers, birds, and leaves. Talk about these things with the children. Then take a walk around the church. Have children watch for the spring things on your list and check them off. This will focus the children's attention and encourage them to observe God's wonderful world more closely.

# Holiday Activities

## 91 Cookie Wreaths

Christmas is a wonderful time to reinforce the idea of sharing with others. Remind the children that God shared His very dearest and precious treasure with us His Son, Jesus! As a fun activity, choose your favorite round, store-bought cookies (butter cookies work well) and let children decorate them with tube type cake decorating icing. Have children share them with another class.

## 92 Prayer Bells

For a Christmas activity that emphasizes our need to help each other by praying, supply children with 5" bell-shaped patterns and construction paper. After children have traced and cut them out, glue a picture of a missionary, friend, or family member on one side. Attach yarn to the bell and hang on the Christmas tree. At family prayer time, you may want to let your child choose one person to pray for.

## 93 Pass the News

This is a version of the old "telephone" game. The players sit in a circle. The first person whispers something into the ear of the person to his or her right such as "Praise God." That person then passes the news on to the person to his or her right and so on. When the message comes back to the last person, he or she says it out loud. The only kind of message the players may pass is good news. (Tip: When playing at Christmastime, the children may be asked to think of Christmas good news such as "God sent Jesus," "Jesus is born," or "It happened in Bethlehem.")

## 94 Wrapping Baby Jesus in Swaddling Clothes

Traditional renditions of the Christmas story—especially those based on the King James Version of the Bible—may tell of Jesus being wrapped in "swaddling clothes" after He was born (Luke 2:7, 12). Modern-day children may be mystified by this reference. Explain that swaddling clothes were like a modern-day baby blanket. In biblical times they were narrow strips of cloth in which a newborn baby was wrapped for warmth and comfort. Provide a doll, a cradle, and strips of soft, white cloth, and let each child take a turn pretending to wrap Baby Jesus in "swaddling clothes," love Him, and then put Him in the "manger." (If possible, embellish the cradle with straw to make it more like a manger.)

## 95 Hide the Ornament

Show an unbreakable Christmas ornament. While everyone closes their eyes, hide the ornament; then tell the children to look for it silently. When they "find" it, they should not point to it or say anything, but just come sit down. When the last person discovers the ornament and sits down, ask the first child who "found" it to show where it was hidden.

## 96 Love Gifts for Jesus

Help children think about ways they can "give gifts of love to Jesus" at Christmastime. Remind them that when we do kind things for others, we are showing love for Jesus.

Older children can help think of ideas, such as: Help clear the supper table; hug someone who needs cheering up; give pennies to church; help pick up toys cheerfully; don't hit back; etc. Write each idea on a slip of paper and put it in a box with wrapping paper on it. (For younger children, write the ideas ahead of time and put them in the box.) Let each child draw out one slip of paper. Read what it says. Encourage each child to do what the paper says this week as a gift of love to Jesus.

## 97 Egg Hunt

Hide paper eggs around the room for the children to find. When they bring an egg to you put a sticker of Jesus on it. Finding eggs is one happy thing to do in spring, but the happiest thing of all is to rejoice because Jesus is alive.

## 98 Thank You, God, for ...

Thanksgiving comes only once a year, but every day we have things for which to be thankful. Children can paste pictures cut from magazines onto heavy paper and make stick figures from the items by attaching to craft sticks. Wave the sticks as you sing these words to the tune **Farmer in the Dell**.

*We give thanks to God.*
*We give thanks to God.*
*God made all things that are good.*
*Thank You, thank You, God.*

## 99 Thank You, God, for Family and Friends

Cut out a string of paper dolls in advance for each child. Have them glue the dolls on a sheet of construction paper. Then let children dress the dolls using fabric scraps, markers, and crayons. As they work on their projects, talk with them about some of the friends God has given them. Remind them to thank God for their friends.

## 100 What's in the Box?

In a box, place classroom items that help your students learn about Jesus. (Teaching-aid figures, books, records or tapes, unbreakable Nativity figures, Christmas cards, and unbreakable ornaments with religious symbols.)

Have your children close their eyes, reach for an item in the bag, and try to guess what the item is.

# 100 Crafts for Ages 3-5

Here are 100 ideas for simple crafts based on simple concepts. Making their own creations will delight children—even if they require a little help from you. Some of these crafts are geared for 2 and 3 year olds, but most are for older children -those who can use scissors and follow simple directions. Some of these suggestions require advance preparation by an adult or adult assistance. To help you prepare for each craft, the materials needed are printed in **bold type**.

Don't forget to praise your children for the effort they put into their projects!

## Bible Story Crafts

### 1 Fish and Net

In Bible times, fishermen used nets instead of poles to catch fish.

*In advance:* Cut out a **cardboard** fish pattern.

Use a **felt-tip marker** to trace the fish pattern onto a **sheet of paper for each child**. Cut six thin strips of paper (11-12" long) for each child. Use different colors of paper to get a netting effect. These strips will form a "fishing net."

Give each child a fish to cut out with blunt-edged **scissors**. Fish can then be glued onto sheets of **blue construction paper**. If desired, the edges of the blue paper can be torn slightly to create an illusion of water.

Then help children **glue** on strips of construction paper so that the strips overlap in a horizontal and vertical manner, giving the appearance of a net. (Some children may actually be able to weave the strips over and under with some assistance.) Optional: Glue on nylon net material or plastic vegetable nets if available.

### 2 Terry Cloth Babies

Give each child a 6" square of **terry cloth**. Cut circles from **construction paper** and let children draw faces on circles, or cut baby faces from appropriate gift wrap. **Paste** a baby's face in one corner of each terry cloth square, then fold the other corners as if wrapping a real baby.

Use these little visual aides when you teach Bible stories involving babies-Samson, Isaac, Samuel, Moses, and Jesus.

### 3 Palm Branches

Give each child a piece of **green construction paper** and show how to fold it in half lengthwise. Then help children round out the two open corners with (blunt-edged) **scissors**. Children may cut slits along the open side, but they should be careful to leave some room between the slits and not to cut through the fold. Unfold for palm branches.

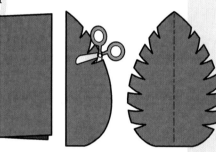

### 4 Kingly Crowns

You'll need:
- [ ] **lightweight cardboard**
- [ ] **stapler, glue**
- [ ] **aluminum foil**
- [ ] **glitter, sequins, etc.**

For each child, provide a strip of cardboard about 2" to 3" wide and long enough to wrap around child's head. Help children cover strips of cardboard by pasting or gluing large pieces of aluminum foil around them.

Decorate crowns with whatever materials you have available. If you add glitter and sequins, *(Continued on next page.)*

you may want them to dry a little before the children wear them. When ready, wrap the crown around the child's head. Staple or tape the ends together so the crowns will be the proper size for each child's head.

Crowns can be worn when acting out stories such as the kind king and the unforgiving servant.

## 5 Noah's Rainbow

Help children **tape** brightly colored **crepe paper streamers** to **paper plates** or cardboard tubes. Show the children how to move their ornaments in an arc to make beautiful, colorful rainbows. You may want to sing or play a record as the children move around the room.

## 6 King Solomon Figure

You'll need:
- [ ] 8 oz. white paper cup
- [ ] construction paper
- [ ] small polystyrene ball
- [ ] colored markers
- [ ] toothpicks
- [ ] 6" chenille wire

*In advance:*
Cut a construction paper crown to fit around the polystyrene ball for each figure.

Give each child a 6-8 oz. white paper (or polystyrene) cup, a chenille wire cut in half, a small polystyrene ball, and a paper crown.

Have each child turn the cup upside down and color Solomon's robe on it with markers. Fashion arms from the chenille wire, folding the hands in front. **Tape** or staple them to the sides of the cup.

Child can then draw a face on the polystyrene ball. Child may want to decorate the crown with **sequins or glitter** before you glue or staple it onto the head. Finally, attach the head to the cup by bringing two or three toothpicks up through the open end of the cup, punching them through the closed end, and up into the polystyrene ball.

## 7 Camels

You'll need:
- [ ] unwaxed paper cups
- [ ] brown paper
- [ ] brown yarn
- [ ] markers, crayons, tape

*In advance:* Cut out camel heads and four 3" strips from brown paper for each set of legs. Draw eyes, mouth, and nose on both sides of each head with a marker.

Give children plain unwaxed paper cups. Let them scribble color on the cups.

Turn cups upside down and help children tape on the camel head and four legs. Bend the legs back as if the camel is kneeling. Tape on brown yarn for a tail.

Have children pretend to ride camels with their fingers. Tell how the wise men rode a long way on their camels to worship baby Jesus.

## 8 Sheep

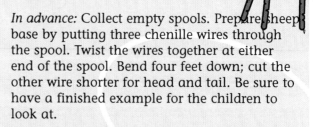

You'll need:
- [ ] empty spools
- [ ] cotton balls
- [ ] chenille wires
- [ ] glue

*In advance:* Collect empty spools. Prepare sheep base by putting three chenille wires through the spool. Twist the wires together at either end of the spool. Bend four feet down; cut the other wire shorter for head and tail. Be sure to have a finished example for the children to look at.

Provide a spool, cotton balls, and glue for each child. Show children how to drop glue on a cotton ball. Place the cotton ball on the spool and hold for a moment to secure. Cover front, back, top, and sides. Place one cotton ball on top of the neck wire. Glue a second ball to that one and shape into a head. Cut small construction paper circles for eyes and ears, and glue onto head.

## 9 Creation Mobile

Provide each child with a **wire coat hanger** and four or five 2-3' **circles cut from tagboard**. (If you can obtain them, small, lightweight plastic lids used for take-out beverages would be ideal for this project.) In the center of each circle, have children place a **sticker** of something God has created: a flower, tree, bird, animal, the sun, or a person. Or, children can cut out small pictures from magazines and glue them onto the circles.

Children will need assistance with the rest of this project. Poke small holes at the top of the circles. Put **thread** through each hole; knot it; then, tie the other end of the string to the bottom of the hanger. Vary the lengths of the threads to give the mobile an interesting appearance.

Children can hang these in their bedrooms as reminders of what God has made.

# Storytelling Crafts

## 10 People Puppets

Cut out the inside circle from **paper plates**. Have children make faces on the paper circles, then **paste** the heads to **craft sticks**.

*For Bible characters:* Have children color hair, beards, or head shawls depending on the story.
*For working people:* Cut out **construction paper** hats representing different kinds of jobs. Have children paste hats on the heads. Use the puppets to act out people working.

## 11 Sad-and-Glad Puppets #1

Provide each child with two **small paper plates** and a wooden **craft stick**. Let children draw sad faces on one of their plates and happy faces on the other. Provide **yarn** to **glue** around the faces for hair. Have children glue the plates back to back with the stick secured in between to form a handle.

Children can hold up the appropriate face as you tell stories of someone who does something wrong . . . then tells God "I'm sorry."

## 12 Sad-and-Glad Puppets #2

Make sad-and-glad puppets from **small paper bags** with fold-over ends. Draw a smiling face on fold-down end. Put body on rest of bag. Under flap, draw sad face. When bag is open, puppet is sad. Bring flap down to make puppet smile.

## 13 Sad-and-Glad Puppets #3

Give each child a piece of **plain paper**, a circle of paper for a face, a half circle (a little larger) for hair, and a **paper fastener** for a nose.

Help the child fasten the circle to the plain paper by pushing the fastener through the center of both. The child may draw two eyes on the circle (the eyes and paper-fastener nose must be in a straight line).

Help the child put **paste** only on the curved edge of the semicircle. Lay the semicircle over the circle, being careful not to let the paste touch the face circle. Let the child draw on a smile. Turn the face circle so the smile disappears beneath the hair. Let the child draw a mouth with the corners turned down.

As you tell a story, children can make the expressions on the face match story characters.

## 14 Flannelboard

Children can make their own flannel boards and flannelgraph pieces. For each child cut a piece of **cardboard** 8 1/2" x 11" and a piece of plain **flannel** slightly larger. Help them **glue** the material to the cardboard. Figures of Jesus and disciples from old **teaching pictures** or people cut from magazines can be backed with construction paper. Glue a small piece of **felt** or sandpaper on the back and the figures will stick to the board. Attach an **envelope** to the back of the board to hold the figures. Be sure child's name is on the board.

## 15 Making a Church

Help children make their own church buildings from boxes. Give each child the **bottom of a small box**. Provide a **pointed paper cup** for each or a cone shape made from a circle of paper. Children may cover the boxes with white paper if desired. Have children turn their boxes upside down and color the windows and a door, then tape the cups or cones on the box bottoms (now the tops) for steeples.

This craft is a good visual for talking about why we come to church and things we can do to take care of God's house.

## 16 Chenille Wire People

*Man or woman:* Use two **chenille wires**. With one wire, make the head and arms. Fasten the second wire to the first at the neck. Shape the second wire into the body and legs. *Child:* Use only one long chenille wire and shape as for adult, only smaller. *Robe:* Cut a hole in the center of a **piece of fabric** 8" x 3". Fit over figure's head; wrap **string or a rubber band** around figure's waist. *Shawl:* Cut a piece of fabric 1 1/2" x 7" in size. Drape it over figure's head, allowing one end to hang down in front. Bring the other end across the front and over the opposite shoulder so it hangs down in back. Fasten in place with a **small safety pin**.

## 17 Chenille Wire Animals

To make a basic animal, use one **chenille wire** for the head and forelegs. Fasten a second wire to the first at the neck and shape this second wire into the body, hind legs, and tail. For a lamb, **glue cotton balls** onto the body. For a donkey, use three wires. The first makes the head and ears; the second makes the fore-legs and body; the third makes the hind legs and tail. A giraffe also requires three wires, one for the head and neck, a second for the forelegs, and a third for the body and hind legs. For an elephant, use four wires. The first makes the trunk and head, the second makes the body, the third makes the forelegs, and the fourth, the hind legs.

## Bulletin Board Crafts

## 18 Friendship Paper Dolls

*In advance:* Fold sheets of **white construction paper** in thirds, like a fan. Cut a simple doll cutout so that when the page is open there are three figures holding hands.

Give one set of figures to each child to color. Then, help children **tape** their figures all around the room. Joining them together at the hands.

## 19 Flower Pictures

*In advance:* Cut three flower stems from **green construction paper** and a square of **red construction paper** (about 5' x 5') for each picture.

Give each child a sheet of construction paper, three flower stems, three pieces of **facial tissue**, and a red square. Help children **glue** the flower stems in the middle of the paper. **Punch** a hole at the top of the flower stems. Twist the facial tissue at the center and pull through the hole from front to back about one inch. **Tape** to the back of the construction paper. Place the square of red paper over the bottom of the stems to look like a flowerpot. Hang the pictures all around the room.

## 20 Self-Portrait Figures

Give children figures cut from **heavy paper** or tagboard to decorate as self-portraits. Children can decorate the figures by coloring them with **crayons** or marking pens to reflect each child's own hair, skin color, and clothing. If you wish, bring in some small **mirrors** so that children can look at their own personal features. *Optional:* Add scraps of yarn for hair and fabric scraps for clothing.

Enjoy how special and different each portrait is—just like each child is special and different.

## 21 Neighborhood Mural

Put up a long piece of **butcher paper** or newsprint. Invite adults from the church to work with the children. Have the adults cut out pictures of people, houses, and other buildings from **magazines** or out of colored paper. Have children draw details such as trees and streets, and **glue** the pictures on the mural. The mural can actually represent the surrounding neighborhood.

Write "Our Neighborhood' on the mural. Hang the mural in the church hall for everyone to see. Hang the mural low enough so that the children can admire their work.

## 22 Star Designs

Give each child a precut **cardboard star** and a piece of **drawing paper**. Have children place their star patterns underneath their papers. Then have them color over the stars to make a textured design as the star shapes appear. Interesting patterns will appear as the star designs overlap. These can be used as a background for a Christmas scene.

## 23 Paper Chain Christmas Tree

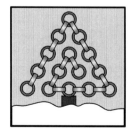

Give each child several 4" **strips of paper** and show how to make a chain by taping the ends of one of the strips together to make a circle, then interlock a second strip of paper to make another circle, until the desired length is reached. **Thumbtack** the chains to a bulletin board so the final result is a triangular Christmas tree. Use a square of **brown construction paper** for a base and **white construction paper** for snow.

## 24 Easter Tree

*In advance:* Prepare a large paper tree, using **green paper**, and attach it to the wall or bulletin board. Also prepare large egg shapes from **colored paper**.

Let each child decorate one or more of the egg shapes, using **crayons**, **glue** and **glitter**, and **sticker stars**. Children may tape their egg shapes to the tree in any position they wish.

## 25 Thank You, God

*In advance:* Make a large cornucopia from **brown paper** and mount it on the bulletin board. Cut out letters to title this display "Thank You, God, for ..."

Provide children with large **paper plates**. Let children draw on the plates the favorite things that they're thankful for, or let them **paste** pictures of those things that they've cut from **magazines**. If they wish, have them decorate their plates with designs, **stickers, colorful leaves,** or **fabric trim.** Assist children in arranging their "thankful" plates on the bulletin board so that they appear to come from the cornucopia.

### Praise and Promises Crafts

## 26 "Special Things" Picture

You'll need:
- [ ] large piece of construction paper or tagboard
- [ ] pictures from magazines
- [ ] a picture of Jesus
- [ ] a picture of each child's family

Have children cut pictures of "special things" from magazines. **Paste** the picture of Jesus in the middle of the large piece of paper. Paste the other pictures carefully to the newspaper. It's okay if they overlap, but don't cover the picture of Jesus.

Children can hang these in their bedrooms to remind them of who and what is special to them.

## 27 Flowers

Let children make flowers to represent the people who help them.

Cut four petals in one shape like a double figure 8 from **construction paper**. Paste two of these on a **craft stick**. Make several of these flowers. Print the names of helpers on the petals or stems: Father, Mother, Brother, Sister, Teacher, Mail Carrier, Police Officer, etc. "Plant" these flowers in **polystyrene or clay** in a **spray can lid or a margarine tub**. Put "Thank You" on the flower pot.

## 28 Church Banks

Give each child a sheet of **construction paper** and an **envelope**. **Paste** the envelope with the flap up onto paper. Decorate the envelope to resemble a church: With **crayons or markers**, draw a door and windows on the bottom section of the envelope; draw a cross above the pointed tip of the flap. Children may keep next Sunday's offering money in their "banks."

## 29 Jesus Mobile

Make a 2 1/2" circle on **white paper** for each child. Draw a 1 1/2" circle inside the 2 1/2" circle. Cut out the center so that you will have a ring. Use the center to make a 1" circle.

Print the Bible verse, "I believe that you are the Son of God–" John 11:27, on the bottom of the ring. Let children color the ring.

Print the word "Jesus" on one side of the 1" circle. Give each child a **sticker picture of Jesus** to place on the other side of the 1" circle.

**Punch** a hole in the top of the 1" circle and near the top and bottom edge of the top of the ring. Thread with a length of knotted **yarn**. Children can hang this mobile in their bedroom to remind them that Jesus is the Son of God.

## 30 Church Building

You'll need:
- [ ] **empty clam-shell box for each child**
- [ ] **construction paper**
- [ ] **chenille wires**
- [ ] **stickers of Jesus; glue**

Help children cut windows and doors from paper. Glue door on the side of the clam-shell box that opens. Glue windows on other sides. Cut chenille wire into two 3" pieces. Twist two wire pieces together to make a cross. Glue cross to top of church near door. Open the box and attach a sticker of Jesus inside.

## 31 Thank You God

Discuss how God made each of us the same: two eyes, a nose, etc. Then discuss how God made each of us different: hair color, size, abilities, etc.

Give each child an 18" **chenille wire**. Show them how to bend and twist it to make the head, body, and legs of a stick-figure person. Add a 6" chenille wire for arms. **Staple** the figure onto a piece of **construction paper** with the title "God created me. Thank You, God."

## 32 God's Care Button

*In advance:* Lightly print "God cares for me" around the inner top edge of a **small paper plate**. Let the children cut off the outside border of the plate so only the center with the printing remains. Then have them trace over the penciled words with a crayon.

Give each child a **happy face sticker** to place on the circle under the words. Then attach a **small safety pin** to the back of the circle with **tape** to pin their buttons to their shirts or dresses.

## 33 Sun Catcher

You'll need:

- [ ] circles precut from white construction paper
- [ ] different colors of tissue paper
- [ ] paste; yarn; hole punch
- [ ] alternative: one plastic lid per child

Give each child a white circle. Place a few sheets of brightly colored tissue paper in the center of the table. Show the children how to tear off a small piece of tissue paper and paste it to the circle. Let the children continue decorating their circles. (*Alternative:* Paste pieces of tissue paper on plastic lids.)

When the project is dry, make a hole in the top; tie a piece of yarn through it. Hang the sun catchers in a window or from the ceiling. The sun catcher can be a reminder that God made beautiful colors for us to enjoy!

## 34 Stained Glass Windows

You'll need:
- [ ] lightweight cardboard
- [ ] black construction paper
- [ ] light colored chalk or crayon
- [ ] small scraps of brightly colored paper

*In advance:* Make a stained glass window pattern (a rectangle with an arching top) from lightweight cardboard. Draw a 1" border around the inside of the pattern; cut out the area inside the border.

Give each child a sheet of black construction paper. Help children trace around the outside and inside edges of the window pattern with a light-colored crayon or chalk. Help children cut along the outside edges of their windows. Let children choose a variety of precut scraps of colored paper—or let them tear their own shapes. Children can **glue** the scraps on the window in a mosaic design, leaving the border as a window frame.

These windows can help remind children that Sunday is a special day to worship God.

## 35 Happy Faces

You'll need:
- [ ] paper plates or precut paper circles
- [ ] small paper circles and semicircles
- [ ] paste or tape; yarn
- [ ] wooden tongue depressors or craft sticks
- [ ] optional: several mirrors

Give each child a paper plate or precut paper circle to be a face. Also, provide each child with smaller paper circles to paste on for the eyes and nose. (Option: Let children look in mirrors as you point out where their facial features are located.) Paste the semicircles on the paper plates to make smiles. Use yarn to make hair. Tape or paste a wooden tongue depressor or craft stick to the back to make handles. Happy faces can be used when singing songs of praise to God.

## 36 My Home and Family

Give each child a sheet of **construction paper**; position it horizontally. Cut off the upper corners to make a house shape. Draw lines to make a roof and four rooms. On each picture print the words, "I thank God for my family." Let children draw their own families in their houses and tell why they're glad for their family.

## 37 Self-Portraits

Tape large sheets of **butcher paper** or newsprint to the floor. Have children take turns lying down on the paper and let other children trace around the bodies of their friends with **crayons**. Then have children color in the outlines of their friends to make life-size self-portraits. Put another sheet of paper behind each figure that has been colored and cut out front and back pieces. Children can also color the back pieces. Then **staple** fronts to backs and stuff with crumpled **newspaper**.

Line up the portraits. Look at all the friends who worked together! Guide children to thank God for their friends.

## 38 Praise Wall Hanging

In Bible times, important people, priests, and kings wore clothes made from purple cloth. Purple cloth was also used in the temple.

*In advance:* Print the words '"We Praise God" on pieces of **purple construction paper**, one for each child.

Have children **glue yarn** or sprinkle glitter on the letters. Fold the top of the paper back one inch. Lay an 18" piece of yarn in the fold and glue or staple the folded flap down; tie the yarn for hanging. Cut the bottom of the construction paper to make fringe.

## Nature Crafts

## 39 Snowflakes

Give each child a square of **white paper**, 5" x 5". Help child fold square into a triangle, then again, then again. With blunt **scissors**, child can cut nicks into the sides of the folded triangle. Unfold. Hang snowflakes in a window with a piece of **tape**, or attach a length of **white thread** to the top of the snowflake and tape the other end of the thread to the top of the window frame.

## 40 Bird Feeder #1

Cut a large opening on each side of a **quart milk carton**. Close the carton at the top and **punch** a hole in the peak. Fasten **cord** through the hole to tie the feeder to a tree branch. Let children put **sunflower seeds** and **bread crumbs** in it. Hang bird feeder on a low tree branch outside a window where children can see it.

## 41 Bird Feeder #2

Help children fill spaces between **pine cone** scales with **peanut butter**, then sprinkle **bird seed** or **bread crumbs** on it. If you do not have pine cones, use a sheet of cardboard. Spread peanut butter on the cardboard and sprinkle bird seed on it. Attach a **string** for hanging the feeder on a tree.

As you work, talk about the fact that birds often have a hard time finding food in winter, and that God is glad when we give them something to eat.

## 42 Pussy Willows

Give each child a sheet of **colored paper**. Help child draw several brown or black lines, which will be branches of pussy willows. Then give the child a number of small pieces of **cotton** to **paste** on the branches for pussy willow buds.

If possible, provide several real pussy willows for children to look at and touch.

## 43 Tulip

1. Fold a 4" square of **red paper** diagonally so that the opposite corners meet to form a triangle.

2. Fold the right corner of the triangle as shown.

3. Fold the left corner of the triangle as shown.

4. Fold the corners toward the back.

5. **Glue or tape** the tulip near the top of a sheet of construction paper.

6. Draw a stem and leaves with **markers**.

## 44 Autumn Trees

Provide each child with a simple tree cut from brown or black **construction paper**. **Paste** tree to piece of paper in a contrasting color. Show children how to tear or cut fall leaves from yellow, red, and orange paper strips. One method: Help children cut heart shapes from the paper, turning the hearts upside down to look like leaves. (Option: Bring in real leaves.) Children may paste or tape their leaves to the free branches.

## 45 'Growing' Flowers

*In advance:* For each child, cut out (1) three bell shapes from **bright-colored paper** for flowers; (2) three green stems; and (3) a yellow circle for a sun. Place a large sheet of construction paper horizontally and cut three slits (the size of the stems) in it, about 2" from the bottom and 4" apart.

1. Give each child the construction paper prepared in advance; position it horizontally with the slits at the bottom. Let child color grass along the bottom.

2. **Paste** the sun in an upper corner of the paper.

3. Show children how to paste the upside-down bell shapes (flowers) to the top of each stem; stick bottom of stem into each slit and pull down.

4. Show child how the flower can "grow" by slowly pulling up on the flower.

## 46 Autumn Picture

You'll need:
- ☐ **pressed autumn leaves**
- ☐ **construction paper**
- ☐ **clear plastic wrap**
- ☐ **tape, scissors, string**

Let each child select a large, colorful autumn leaf and tape it on construction paper. Help child tape a piece of clear plastic wrap over the leaf to keep it from falling off. Then frame picture with strips of construction paper. Tape a loop of string to the top or back and child will have a nature picture ready to hang.

## 47 Spring Appreciation

Give each child a 9" x 12" piece of **green construction paper** folded in half horizontally. Help child cut through the fold, extending the cuts from the fold to an inch away from the opposite edge. Make cuts about 1/2" apart all along the fold to resemble grass.

The let each child draw several tulip shapes with stems on **colored construction paper**. Be sure to leave a 1" border at the bottom of each stem connecting all the tulip shapes. After the children cut out the flowers, position the border along the uncut edge of the grass and help them roll the grass and flowers together. The grass should be on the outside with the flowers sticking out of the top. **Tape** the edges so that the grass will not unroll.

## Crafts to Give

### 48 "Jesus Loves You" Basket

Show children how to ...

1. Lick the flap shut on a **business-size envelope**.

2. Fold the envelope in half lengthwise.

3. Beginning on one side, cut away the open edges halfway down the length of the envelope to make a pretty handle (see illustration). Unfold.

4. Decorate the basket and handle with **crayons, stickers, glitter, sequins**, etc. Print "Jesus Loves You" on one side.

5. Spread apart the sides of the envelope to open up basket.

6. Fill the basket with treats (**candy** or **flowers**) and give to a friend. Tell your friend that Jesus loves him or her and you do, too!

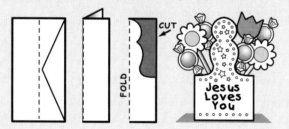

### 49 Bookmarks

Child can make several bookmarks to give as gifts to family members to put in their Bibles.

Provide **construction paper strips** about 1 1/2" by 5".

Let child place a **sticker seal** of Jesus at the top of each strip. At the bottom, print "Jesus loves (Mother, Daddy, Becky)" to personalize each bookmark. For more durable bookmarks, cover the fronts and backs with a clear adhesive-backed plastic.

### 50 Gift Baskets

Give each child an empty **cottage cheese or margarine container**. Cover the outside with colorful **tissue paper; tape or glue** in place and attach a **self-stick bow**. Children may put **fruit, crayons**, or **a small toy** in the basket to give as a gift.

### 51 Sponge-Painted Tray

You'll need:
- [ ] **fiber vegetable trays or egg carton tops**
- [ ] **spring-type clothespins**
- [ ] **sponges; tempera paint; aluminum muffin tins**

Each child will need a fiber vegetable tray (ask at the produce department of the grocery store) or a fiber egg carton top. (Do not use polystyrene since tempera will not adhere properly.)

Cut "holey" sponges into 1 1/2" pieces. Clip a clothespin to each sponge piece. Pour a small amount of tempera paint into aluminum muffin tins. Let child dip the sponge into the paint and dab it on the tray. Provide each child with one sponge for each color, otherwise the paint will become muddy. Allow the trays to dry thoroughly.

Discuss things that could be kept in the tray: crayons, jewelry, pencils, odds and ends.

### 52 Carnations

For each flower, cut **facial tissues** into four 4"-diameter circles. Place a **button** on the center of the circles; thread a knotted yarn through the button and layers of tissue. Pull **yarn** through a slit in a **sheet of paper; tape** yarn down on the back of the paper. Then crumple each layer of tissue around the button. Draw a stem and leaves with a crayon. (Option: Spray perfume on the flowers.) Children can take the flowers to lonely or ill friends.

## 53 Vase and Flowers

You'll need:
- ☐ empty spool
- ☐ 3 toothpicks; glue
- ☐ lace or ribbon
- ☐ construction paper

*In advance:* Cut three small flower shapes from construction paper for each child. Print the word "I" on one flower, "AM" on the next flower, and "SORRY!" on the third flower.

Show children how to glue ribbon or lace around the middle of the spool. Place a small amount of glue on the end of each toothpick and allow children to stick it on their flowers. A small wad of paper should be placed in each spool before arranging the "flowers."

The gift can be given to a friend or a family member when the child needs to say, "I'm sorry."

## 54 Paper Bag Basket

Cut 5" off the open end of a **lunch bag** for each basket. Let child decorate the sides of the bag with designs, using construction **paper scraps**, **glue**, and **crayons**. Help child use **scissors** to make a scalloped edge along the top of the bag.

Cut a strip from the discarded top of the paper bag, about 1 1/4" wide and 12" long. Tape to the sides of the decorated basket for a handle. Fill with **flowers, peanuts, candies,** or a **small gift** to give to a friend.

## 55 Get Well Pockets

*In advance:* Cut **paper plates** in half. Provide each child with a whole paper plate and one of the halves. Let each child decorate the plates (front side of whole plate; back side of half plate) with **crayon** designs. Write "Get Well Soon!" on the container.

**Staple** a half plate to a whole plate to make a pocket container. **Punch** a hole at the top and lace **yarn** through each plate so it can hang on the wall.

Explain that a sick friend or relative can use the pocket for tissues, a pad of paper and a pencil to write notes, or to keep get-well cards in.

## 56 Cone Baskets

Let children scribble color a piece of **construction paper**. Roll the paper into cone shapes and **staple or tape** the sides to make a basket. Tape a **chenille wire** handle on each basket. Let the children put things in their baskets, such as **wild flowers** or small **plastic bags** filled with **nuts** and **raisins**, to give to a special person.

## 57 Christmas Paperweight

You'll need:
- ☐ baby food jars; construction paper
- ☐ stones to fill jars; paste or glue
- ☐ optional: glitter, wrapping paper

Give each child a red or green paper rectangle cut to fit around a baby food jar. Let child paste on scraps of torn construction paper to decorate the rectangle. (*Option:* Glue on glitter or small pictures cut from wrapping paper.)

After decorating the paper rectangle, paste it around the baby food jar. Fill the jar with small stones—be careful not to break the jar. Have children give this paperweight as a Christmas gift to grandparents or friends.

Vary this gift idea for any time of the year by decorating the paperweight in appropriate ways.

## 58 Photo Gift

*In advance:* Take **pictures of each child** and get them developed. Print "Happy Mother's Day," or other appropriate words, at the top of a sheet of **construction paper**. **Punch** holes about 1" apart around entire paper. Cut pieces of **yarn** 1 1/2 yards long. Wrap **masking tape** around yarn ends so it will go through holes easily.

Have children **glue** their photographs under the writing on their papers, and write their names underneath. Starting at the top, center, show them how to thread yarn in and out through the holes around the outside of the papers. Tie ends in a bow at top.

## 59 Gift Sachets

Sachets can be hung in closets to make clothes smell nice.

Give each child a sheet of **green or red construction paper** measuring 2" x 4". Guide children in folding the paper in half; **staple** the sides closed. Help children sprinkle a few drops of **perfume or cologne** on a **cotton ball**. (Children might want to make two sachets-one using perfume for mother and the other using after-shave for father.) Place the cotton ball inside the sachet pocket.

With a **paper punch**, punch a hole at the top of the sachet through the front and back sides. Loop a piece of yarn through the hole and tie the sachet closed. Tie the ends of the **yarn** to make a loop so that the sachet can be hung up. **Stickers** can be added to the front and back of the sachet for decoration.

## 60 Butterfly Bookmarks

For each butterfly bookmark, provide a 1" x 7" strip of colored construction paper and a simple butterfly shape cut from white paper. Print the words "I love you" on the strip of **colored construction paper**.

Cover the worktable with **newspaper**. Let children color their butterflies, then help them spread a thin coat of **glue** on the butterfly and sprinkle **glitter** on the glue. Shake the butterfly gently over the newspaper to remove the excess glitter. Glue the butterfly to one end of the strip of paper.

I love you

## 61 Father's Day Gift Ideas

*Scribble pictures.* Children may scribble-color pictures on **drawing paper** and paste black **paper strips** around them to make a frame.

*Pencil cans.* Cut heavy **gift-wrap paper or adhesive-backed shelf paper** to fit around **empty soup cans** (be sure there are no sharp edges); **tape** in place.

*Paper weights.* Children can make paper weights by painting **rocks** with **tempera paint**. Let rocks dry; show how to make designs with a different color. **Shellac** if possible.

## 62 Hand Plaques

Roll out **play dough** or clay 1/2" thick in a colorful **paper plate**. Press child's hand into the clay to make imprint. Place a **ribbon** on the back of the plate for hanging purposes. When dry, place each plaque in a **paper bag** and tie a ribbon around the top of the bag. These can be given as presents for mother or father.

## 63 My Book ... for You

Give children **crayons** and some sheets of **paper**. Have them draw several pictures of a sun, tree, flower, bird, family, house, pets, toys.

When drawings are finished, stack them neatly. Put a fresh sheet of paper on the top and on the bottom to make a cover. **Staple** books along the side. Or **punch** two holes in the book and tie together with **yarn**. Write "MY BOOK by. . ." and child's name on the cover.

Grandmother would love to receive this gift!

## Just for Fun Crafts

## 64 Place Mats

Help children weave place mats by putting narrow strips of **construction paper or wallpaper** in and out of slits cut evenly in a different colored sheet of construction paper.

## 65 Snowman 1

You'll need:
- ☐ **marshmallows**
- ☐ **toothpicks**
- ☐ **polystyrene square**
- ☐ **raisins**

Give each child three marshmallows and a polystyrene square. Show children how to make snowmen by sticking the marshmallows together with toothpicks. Put two marshmallows together with one toothpick. Stick another toothpick halfway into the bottom marshmallow, then place the third marshmallow on this toothpick. Stick a third toothpick into the polystyrene base and push the snowman onto the toothpick, so the snowman will stand. Two more toothpicks can be used for arms sticking out of the middle marshmallow. Use pieces of toothpicks to add raisin eyes and mouth to the top marshmallow.

## 66 Snowman 2

Use a **paper plate** to make this happy snowman! Draw a line around the perimeter of the plate, one inch from the outer rim, leaving a 2" section blank at the top. Now draw another circle 2" inside the first one: leave a 2" section blank on this line as well, directly opposite from the first blank section. Cut along the lines. Do not cut where the blank sections are.

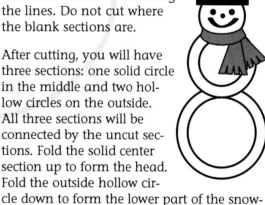

After cutting, you will have three sections: one solid circle in the middle and two hollow circles on the outside. All three sections will be connected by the uncut sections. Fold the solid center section up to form the head. Fold the outside hollow circle down to form the lower part of the snowman's body. The middle hollow circle will form the middle of the snowman's body. Decorate the top circle with **construction paper** features and a hat and scarf.

## 67 Finger Painting Fun

Children will love the feel and effect of making things in paint with their fingers. Provide **smocks** from old shirts to protect their clothes, and cover the work surface with **newspapers**. Be sure to dip the **paper** in **water** before you put paint on the paper. Help children use their fingers and hands in various ways to make different things in their pictures.

Here's a recipe for **finger paint** or it can be purchased at a craft or toy store:

1. Mix 1 1/2 cups cold-water **starch** with 1 1/2 cups **soap flakes**.

2. Slowly stir in 2 cups of cold water, stirring until the mixture is smooth and thick.

3. Add **powdered tempera paint** to make the colors you choose.

## 68 House Painting

Children enjoy painting pictures of their houses. Or they might like to paint pictures of different kinds of houses: tall apartments, long ranch houses, grass huts, igloos, tepees, etc.

Use **washable paint**, such as tempera or even finger paint. Twist **cotton** around the end of **toothpicks (or use cotton swabs)** to make paintbrushes. Dip brushes in tempera paint and let children paint pictures on construction paper.

## 69 My Own Watch

Watch pattern: Make a pattern for a paper watch by tracing a quarter for the watch face. Now draw a band about 1/2" wide and 2 1/2" long on each end of the watch face. (Total length of watch-about 6 1/2 inches.)

Trace the watch pattern onto **white construction paper**. Let child color the watch. After you have drawn the numbers, insert a **paper fastener** in the center of the watch face to serve as hands. One inch from one end of the band, make a slit halfway into the watchband; do the same thing at the other end except on the opposite side. Wrap the watch around child's wrist, insert the slits into one another, and secure with tape.

The watch can be a reminder that God looks after us all the time!

## 70 Train Picture

*In advance*: Cut several rectangles and small circles out of **colored paper**. Show children how to **paste** several rectangles close together on a sheet of **construction paper** to form the train cars, using the small circles as wheels. Long strands of **uncooked spaghetti** can be glued under the train to make train tracks.

## 71 Birds

You'll need:
- [ ] **circles, small triangles, ovals, and strips precut from construction paper**
- [ ] **paste; crayons; hole punch**
- [ ] **optional: small craft feathers**
- [ ] **yarn pieces 24" long**

Give each child a precut circle, triangle, and oval. Show them how to paste the three shapes together to form a bird-the oval for a body, the circle for a head, and the small triangle for a beak. Child can scribble color a bird, then draw eyes on the bird's head. For a tail, paste on strips of colored paper (or small craft feathers).

When birds are finished punch a hole in the top and loop a piece of yarn through it. Decorate the room by hanging the birds from the ceiling. The birds can be a reminder to thank God for all the good things He has made.

## 72 "Feather" Duster

Make a "feather" duster for helping at home. The duster may be made from a 12" length of **newspaper**. Cut in shreds to a depth of 4 inches. Roll tightly and fasten with **tape**.

This feather duster may actually be used, so let children dust the Sunday school or children's church room, or use it at home to dust their rooms.

## 73 House "Rubbing"

Show children how to make a picture of a house with the texture of a building material. Have children place a piece of **typing paper** over a brick, a stucco wall, or a piece of weathered wood. **Tape** paper to the object to prevent it from moving. Children should color with the side of a **crayon** so that the texture of the material shows on the paper.

Now cut out the silhouette of a house from a sheet of **construction paper**, leaving the four sides of the construction paper as a frame. Place texture behind the frame, filling the cutout shape. **Paste** in place.

## 74 Sailboat

Let each child mold a boat from **clay or play dough**. Cut one **straw** in half. Help child **tape** a triangle of paper to a piece of straw to make the sail. Stick the sail in the middle of the boat. Add oars to the boat by cutting the other piece of straw in half again and putting them in the boat's sides.

## 75 Litter Bag

Give each child a **brown lunch bag** to decorate for a litter bag. Provide large **crayons** for drawing mountains, lakes, and flowers. Or, from **magazines** cut nature pictures that can be **glued** on the bags.

Use the litter bag to pick up litter as you walk outdoors ... or use it for clean-up time in the classroom ... or suggest children keep the litter bag in the family car.

## 76 Thumbprint Pictures

Give each child a half sheet of **light-colored construction paper**. Press your thumb onto a **stamp pad** and make two thumbprints on the page. These prints will be the mother and father cats.

Now let each child press his or her thumb onto the stamp pad and make three or four thumbprints next to yours. Child can then draw ears, whiskers, and tails on the cats with **felt-tip pens**. Or, provide **yarn or string** to **glue** on the page for tails.

## 77 Marshmallow House

You'll need:

- ☐ 9" x 12" construction paper
- ☐ 5" x 3" construction paper
- ☐ 12 toothpicks; 8 miniature marshmallows

Place each child's building materials on a 9" x 12" piece of construction paper. (The house can be carried more easily by leaving it on the sheet of construction paper.) Show how to build a foundation for the structure by joining four toothpicks and four marshmallows to form a square. Use four toothpicks to build up the walls. Then form the ceiling by adding four marshmallows and four toothpicks, forming a cube. Fold the 5" x 3" construction paper in half and set it on the structure for a roof. Use **glue** to hold in place.

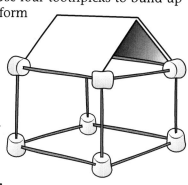

## 78 Butterfly

Give each child a sheet of **colored tissue paper** about 8 1/2" x 12". Help child fold the paper in half horizontally.

Give each child a **twist tie** such as those included in boxes of trash bags. Place the tie around the center of the folded paper and twist once or twice tightly. The tissue paper should gather and form butterfly wings on both sides of the tie. Bend the ends of the tie to form antennae.

Decorate the wings by gluing on small pieces of brightly colored paper.

## 79 Japanese Lantern

Fold a sheet of **colored paper** in half vertically. Starting on the folded edge, cut strips about 1/2" wide and not quite to the edge of the paper. Unfold the paper and join the ends so slits are vertical on the lantern. Then **staple** a paper handle to the top of the lantern. Hang the lanterns from the ceiling with **string** or thread for room decorations.

## 80 Mouse

You'll need:
- [ ] **construction paper**
- [ ] **paper punch; scissors**
- [ ] **cotton bails; yarn**
- [ ] **tape or glue**

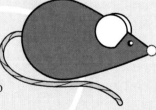

*In advance:* For each mouse body, cut a sheet of construction paper into a large teardrop shape; also precut two rounded ears.

Give a teardrop shape to each child. The pointed end will be the mouse's nose and the rounded end will be where its tail is attached. Give each child two precut, rounded ears. Show how to paste or tape the ears to both sides of the mouse's body. With a paper punch, punch out small paper circles for eyes. Let child glue on tiny cotton ball for nose and a piece of yarn for the tail.

## 81 Ice Cream Cone

Give each child a piece of **brown construction paper** about 6" x 6" square. Roll and **tape** the square into a cone shape to resemble an ice-cream cone.

Now give each child a sheet of **tissue paper** and show how to wad it up into a ball (the "ice cream"). **Glue** or tape "ice cream" into the cone.

## 82 Fish

Give each child a large sheet of **paper**. Let child tear it into a fish shape, and then scribble **color** it. With the point of a pair of **scissors**, make a small hole in the end of the fish. Put one end of a piece of **string** through the hole and tie a knot in it right in front of the hole. Now child has a fish that can be taken for a "swim" by being pulled around the room.

## Crafts for Special Days

## 83 Stuffed Turkeys

Draw a fat turkey body (front view) on **construction paper** and cut it out. Wad up a piece of paper and **glue** it to the back of the turkey. Place turkey on a piece of construction paper for background and glue in place. Cut feathers from construction paper and glue on background.

## 84 Pilgrim Hats

Use white **polystyrene drinking cups** to make pilgrim hats. Place cups on a **cookie sheet**. Put into a preheated oven at 350 degrees for 12 to 15 seconds. The cups will shrink to look like miniature hats. Let children decorate with **paint, ribbon,** and **foil**. These little hats make great party favors.

## 85 Yarn Turkey

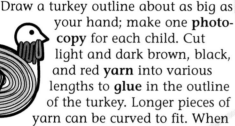

Draw a turkey outline about as big as your hand; make one **photocopy** for each child. Cut light and dark brown, black, and red **yarn** into various lengths to **glue** in the outline of the turkey. Longer pieces of yarn can be curved to fit. When the yarn picture is finished, cut out and glue the yarn turkey to a piece of construction paper.

## 86 Apple Turkeys

You'll need:
- [ ] **apples, raisins**
- [ ] **frosting**
- [ ] **cardboard**
- [ ] **large marshmallows**
- [ ] **toothpicks**
- [ ] **crayons or markers**

Cut a fan-shaped tail from cardboard for each turkey; let children color the tail any way they wish. Slice into apple about halfway down from the top; on one side of the apple insert tail into cut. Attach marshmallow (the head) to the other side of the apple with a toothpick. Spread frosting on the end of the marshmallow and place raisins for the eyes, nose, and mouth in the frosting.

## 87 Hand-y Tree

Draw outlines of children's hands on **red, green, or white construction paper**. Cut out the outlines, and write a child's name on each cutout. (One child could make several.)

Make a base for the tree by rolling a large piece of flexible **cardboard** into a cone shape. Stand it upright. Starting at the bottom, **staple** or tape hand cutouts over the base. Place a star at the top and you have a holiday decoration that everyone helped make!

If you have a large group of children or would like this to be a project for the entire Sunday school, make the cone-shaped base large.

## 88 Memory Tree

A memory tree is a great way to remember every student you've taught. Prior to the holidays, have children cut out pretty shapes from **colored poster board or construction paper** and **paste** their school pictures on them. Using a **hole punch**, punch a hole through the picture ornament. Thread a colorful **ribbon or** piece of **yarn** through the hole.

A few weeks before Christmas hang the ornaments of previous classes and the current class on an artificial free.

## 89 Christmas Place Mats

Help children trace around **Christmas cookie cutters** to make pretty designs on **red or green construction paper** for holiday place mats. Help the children attach large **star stickers** or other Christmas stickers to their place mats.

# 90 Play-Dough Fun

You'll need:
- [ ] 1 cup flour
- [ ] 1 tablespoon oil
- [ ] 2 teaspoons cream of tartar
- [ ] 10 drops food coloring in 1 cup water
- [ ] 1/2 cup salt
- [ ] dash mint extract

Mix above ingredients in saucepan; stir and cook until mixture is the consistency of mashed potatoes and forms a ball. Knead until cool. Store in airtight container. Enough for 8 to 10 children.

Give children play dough and suggest that they make something that reminds them of the birth of Jesus. Provide cookie cutters to cut stars or sheep, or let children form baby Jesus, Mary, shepherds, wise men, or camels from the dough.

# 91 Christmas Bells

You'll need:
- [ ] polystyrene cups
- [ ] rickrack
- [ ] aluminum foil
- [ ] star stickers
- [ ] jingle bells (optional)
- [ ] glue or paste
- [ ] glitter
- [ ] chenille wires
- [ ] gold cord or yarn

Turn foam cups into bells by covering them with foil or by spreading a thin coat of glue on the cups and adding rickrack and stars or by sprinkling the cups with glitter.

Use a chenille wire to make the bell clapper. Punch a hole in the top of the cup, insert the chenille wire, and make a small loop at both ends. Attach a length of gold cord or yarn in the top loop for a hanger. Or, attach a jingle bell to the chenille wire clapper so the bell will really ring.

# 92 Star Decoration 1

Give each child a **construction paper** star. Have ready **tissue paper** cut into 1" squares. Show children how to crumple each piece of tissue paper into a little ball. Cover each star with dots of **glue**: add the tissue-paper balls to cover the star. With a **paper punch**, punch a hole in one of the points of the star. Loop a piece of **yarn** through the hole so the star may be hung up.

# 93 Star Decoration 2

Give each child two **white paper** stars traced from a pattern. (Cut out the stars ahead of time or let children do it.) Place one star on the table in front of each child and put a dot of **glue** in the center. Place the other star on top so the points are matching, but only the centers are glued together. Help children decorate both sides of the star with **crayons** or **glitter**. Fold the points of the star away from each other so it is three-dimensional. Attach a **string** to the star between two points for hanging.

# 94 Christmas Story Ornaments

You'll need:
- [ ] used Christmas cards with religious scenes
- [ ] lids from plastic containers

With a **black marker**, trace a circle on each card so that when the card is trimmed the picture will fit inside a plastic lid. The edge of the lid will provide a frame. Children can choose the picture they want and cut along the black line. Help them **glue** the picture to the lid, and, with a **paper punch**, make a hole at the top of the pictures. Loop a piece of **yarn** through the hole and tie the ends.

# 95 Angel Decoration

You'll need:
- [ ] 8 1/2" X 11" white paper
- [ ] tape
- [ ] 3" chenille wire
- [ ] glitter, yarn, trim
- [ ] small white paper circle

Have a finished angel for children to look at as they do the project step by step.

1. A circle of white paper will be the angel's head. Add the face and hair with crayons or bits of yarn.

2. Decorate the 8 1/2"\ x 1 1" paper body of the angel with fabric trim, glitter, or crayons. Then accordion fold the body.

3. Tape the chenille wire to the head and insert between pleats at one end of the body. Press the pleats together around the chenille wire and secure with tape or staples,

4. When the pleats at the other end are fanned out the angel will stand up. You can also attach a string behind the head and form a loop to hang up each.

# 96 Manger Scene

You'll need:
- [ ] plain paper cups
- [ ] nut cups
- [ ] cotton
- [ ] fine-point markers
- [ ] 2 sizes small polystyrene balls
- [ ] bits of dark yarn
- [ ] fabric scraps
- [ ] glue; tape
- [ ] sturdy cardboard

Let each child make a different figure: Mary, Joseph, two shepherds, a sheep, baby Jesus.

*For each person:* Use an upside-down paper cup, with an upside-down nut cup glued on top of it. Glue dark yarn for hair and beards to foam ball; glue ball to bottom of nut cup. Draw features with fine-point markers. Use fabric scrap for Mary's head covering.

*To make a sheep:* Glue cotton on an upside-down nut cup. Add smallest foam ball for the head.

*To make baby Jesus:* Stuff cotton into nut cup; use smallest foam ball tucked into cotton for head.

Make a simple manger from cardboard. To fasten paper cup figures to the board, put a long strip of tape inside the cup so that it makes a U-shape, with the bottom of the U across the open mouth of the cup. The sides of the U adhere to the sides of the cup; the bottom of the U should fasten to the board.

# 97 Christmas Wreath

You'll need:
- [ ] green poster board
- [ ] small hard candies
- [ ] red ribbon
- [ ] paste

*In advance:* Cut out a Christmas wreath for each child. Make a pattern by cutting a small circle from the center of a larger circle. Cut the wreaths from green tagboard or heavy paper.

Let children paste candies and red ribbon bows on their wreaths.

## 98 Button Valentine

Each child will need a **large button** to which you have sewn a **safety pin** (leaving the point of the pin part free). Each child will also need a **construction paper** heart, a little larger than the button, on which the words "I Love You" have been printed.

To decorate: Spread a little **glue** around the outside of the heart and let the child sprinkle **glitter** on it. Child can then glue the construction paper heart to the button. When the glue is dry, pin the button on the child's coat. Some children may want to give away their buttons as valentine gifts.

## 99 Lily Pictures

Give each child a half piece of **construction paper** and six white, leaf-shaped petals. Show children how to roll one end of each petal around a **pencil** to make it curl. **Paste** the petals in a circle with flat ends touching and curled ends out so that the petals form a single lily. Use **crayons** to add stems and leaves.

## 100 Tomb Picture

Give each child a **large paper plate**. Cut a straight section off the bottom so the plate is horseshoe-shape. This will represent the tomb. Draw a rectangular doorway and color the inside black. Color the rest to look like the stone tomb.

Now give each child the center circle cut from a **smaller paper plate**, large enough to cover the doorway. Attach this on the right side of the circle and doorway with a **paper fastener**.

Now child can see the tomb closed, then roll away the stone to see that the tomb is empty. Jesus is not there anymore; Jesus is alive!

# 100 Indoor Games for Ages 3-5

A room full of children means a room full of energy. This section is loaded with games that will help you use that energy to praise God and learn more about His love. Just a quick look through these fresh game ideas will make planning a time with children easy for any setting: home, school, church, anywhere! And keep this handy for those times when you need an on-the-spot idea.

## Getting to Know You

### 1 I Spy a Special Person

Play a version of "I Spy" called "I Spy a Special Person." When playing this game, children can highlight positive features about other children such as hair color, eye color, clothing. The leader demonstrates by saying something like "I spy a special person who is wearing blue stripes." The children can raise their hands to guess who the special person is. The child who guesses correctly gets to be the next one to choose the special person. Each child should be chosen at least once as you emphasize that God has made everyone wonderful and unique.

### 2 What's My Name?

Sitting in a circle, children say their own name aloud just before rolling the ball to another person in the circle. Encourage eye contact so that they will know when they will be receiving the ball. The game may be played again later with the child calling the name of another child in the circle before rolling the ball to that person. This will introduce them to the group and help them to learn the names of other children.

### 3 Meet My Friend

Here is a game that will help children become better acquainted. Hide pairs of different colored happy faces around the room. When the leader says "GO!" the children search for one face. When two children find the same color they become partners. They are then to find out their partner's name and favorite animal. When the group comes back together, each child can introduce his or her partner.

### 4 Group Hug!

Play music as children move around the room. Direct their movement with directions such as tip-toe, skip, hop, crawl, etc. When the music stops, each child finds someone to hug, saying "Jesus loves you!" Repeat with instructions for groups of three to hug, then four, etc. The kids may make a new friend as they share Jesus' love through hugs!

### 5 Touch That Color!

This game is another opportunity for children to get to know each other and to remind them of all the fun colors that God has made. Place children in pairs or small groups. The leader calls out, "Touch something red (or another color)!" and each child must touch a piece of their partner's clothing that is the color the leader called out.

## 6 Name Game

This simple rhythm game will help children to learn each other's names and become more comfortable with new friends.

Have children sit in a circle and establish a simple rhythm by patting thighs and clapping alternately, or by patting knees alternately. Once the rhythm is established, all chant together: "I have a good friend, _____ is his/her name," with children taking turns filling in their names until everyone has been introduced.

Variation for older children: As the children become more confident, you might have each individual recite these two lines in rhythm: "My name is _____, and my eyes are _____." (or, "and my hair is _____" or "and I like _____"); then the rest of the class echoes the lines back to the child who first recited them. ("Her name is Karen, and she likes spaghetti.")

## 7 Stumped!

To help children learn the names of the others in their group, have everyone sit in a circle. Go around the circle and have each child tell his or her first name. After the child says his or her name, the group must think of an action that starts with the same sound as the child's name (e.g. Jim-jump, Lauren-laugh, Marissa-mop). The leader may have to help the kids identify the first sound in the name before they can think of an action. The child must then do that action. If the group is stumped and can't think of an action to go with the name, everyone in the group must roll up in a ball like a tree stump, and say, on the count of three, "We're stumped!"

## 8 Color Match

This matching game will help kids get moving among other children while working on recognizing their colors and shapes. In advance, cut out pairs of shapes from different colors of construction paper. Be sure that every shape has a match (both color and shape should be the same.) Tape the shapes to the backs of half the kids and tell the kids that they cannot take them off or look at them. Give the other shapes to kids and allow them to look at them. They must then go and find the child who has the shape that matches theirs. Tell them to make sure both the shape and the color are the same. When a child thinks that he or she has found a matching shape, that child and the child with the match should walk over to a designated wall. They can then take the shape off the back of the child, make sure it really is a match, and then hold the shapes up in front of them. If the children decide that the two really don't match exactly, they should place one of the shapes on the child's back again and return to the group to find the correct pairs. If the shapes do match exactly, the pair should stand together, holding up their shapes until everyone has found their match.

## 9 Animal Intro

Children sit in a circle. Each chooses an animal that he or she would like to be. Each child needs to choose a different animal so that no children have the same animal name. Then have them choose and demonstrate a motion for their animal (arm as trunk for elephant, wag hand as a tail for dog, clap hands together for crocodile, etc.). Go around the circle and have each child tell the name of their animal and demonstrate their animal's motion. The leader starts the game by making his or her own animal motion and then the animal motion of another person. That person must then make his or her motion and another. If a child gets stumped and can't think of another animal motion, or does not make his or her own animal motion first, that child must get up and walk one time around the outside of the circle, making the motions and sounds of his or her animal. That child then sits back down in the circle and the person to his or her left starts play again by making his or her own animal motion and then one of another child in the group.

## 10 Name Train

The leader begins this game by going up to a child and saying, "Name train, name train, what's your name?" The child answers, telling the leader his or her name. The leader then repeats the child's name, imitating the way it was said (thud or soft voice, accent, etc.), "Jesse... Jesse, Jesse-Jesse-Jesse." (This can get fun when the children realize you will imitate the way they say their name!) That child then stands behind the leader with his or her hands on the leader's waist forming the beginning of the Name Train. The child that is now part of the train joins the leader in asking the children their names and repeating the names as they are said. Each child is added to the back of the train until everyone is part of the name train. Encourage the children to wrap the train around each child as they ask him or her to join the train so that the child feels welcomed by all and so that the people at the back of the train remain just as much a part of the game as those at the front.

## 11 Name Tug-of-War

Divide the group into two teams. Have all the members of both teams stand in a circle around a pillow. Each child should hold onto a part of a pillow. (If there are too many kids to hold onto one pillow, divide them again and have some play a second round.) At the leader's signal, the children must pull the pillow over a designated point for their team. The team that wins the tug-of-war gets to go first in the "naming" part of the game. For this part of the game, the two teams are to line up facing each other. The team that won the tug-of-war should start the game by saying the name of one of the kids on the opposite team. Have the teams go back and forth saying the name of one person on the other team. The teams are not allowed to repeat someone's name for more than one turn. The team that knows the most names of kids on their opposing team wins. Mix the children up, divide them into new teams, and play again. Soon the kids will know all the names of those in their group!

## 12 Grape mania

The story from Matthew 21:28-32 is about a father who asks his two sons to help him work in the vineyard, but only one son obeys his father. For a fun game to go along with this story, label two cardboard boxes with the word "grapes." Prior to the game, have all the children crumple up more than enough pieces of paper to fill both boxes.

Place all the crumpled "grapes" in one spot, some distance from the boxes and divide the group of children into two teams. At the leader's signal, have each team work together to try to fill their team's box first.

## 13 Remember the Lord's Supper

Have the children sit in a circle around a tablecloth set with the following items: place mat, napkin, cup, plate, round loaf of bread, juice pitcher. The children should cover their eyes while the child who is "It" removes one item from the tablecloth and moves the remaining items around. The children can then uncover their eyes, and the first child to raise his or her hand and guess the missing object becomes "It." The game is over when all the items have been removed or each child has been "It." Remind the group that Jesus ate the Lord's Supper with His disciples (Luke 22:14-20) and asked them to remember Him each time they ate this special meal.

## 14 David Not Afraid!

Children love to play games relating to the courage that God gave David in facing Goliath! Have children crouch on the ground with one student, selected to be David, holding five clumps of loosely wadded newspaper where Goliath can't see them. Another student, selected as Goliath, walks among the crouched children and says, "I'm a giant big and tall, you can't get me, you're too small." Then Goliath freezes and David stands up, says, "I'm David. I'm not afraid!" and throws the newspaper at Goliath. If David hits Goliath, David becomes the new giant and another David is chosen. If the child misses Goliath, new children are chosen to be both David and Goliath. Discuss how God gave David the courage to face Goliath (1 Samuel 17).

## 15 Jonah and the Whale

Start this relay race with the first runners from each team sitting on a pile of pillows (the boat). To get through the course they must do a somersault or roll off of the pillows, and crawl underneath a sheet (held waist high by two people who shake it to simulate waves in the ocean). Finally, they must crawl through a long refrigerator box with a whale painted on the side and then run back to their team and tag the next runner. The first team to have everyone complete the course successfully and be seated at the starting line wins.

## 16 Race for the Ark

Choose one child to be Noah and assign one leader as Noah's assistant. The two of them should walk down a line of the other children and whisper the name of an animal in each child's ear. Be sure that each animal is assigned twice so there will be a pair to board the ark. Then Noah says, "The rain is coming! Hurry and come to the ark!" All the children should then start making their animal sound and walking, crawling, or slithering around trying to find their mate. When a match is found, they head to "the ark" (two chairs with a blanket draped between them) and crawl through the door. Try to see how quickly you can get all the animals safely inside and serve animal crackers as a reward.

## 17 Lion's Den

One child, chosen as the lion, goes to his den in the center of the circle of other children. With everyone on all fours, have the circle of children say, "Lion, lion, let's make a deal! Whoever you catch can be your next meal!" Then the lion leaves its den and crawls after the others. Once a child is tagged they must go sit in the lion's den. The last one to be caught is the lion for the next game. It would be scary to be chased by a real lion! But God protected Daniel in the lion's den (Daniel 6:19-22).

## 18 Moses, Moses

Place two jump ropes on the floor parallel to one another. One child stands between them as Moses and the others line up behind one of the ropes. Children say, "Moses, Moses,may we cross the sea?" Moses responds with, "If you are wearing (color, type of clothing, etc.), you will be safe." All children who fit that description may cross to the other side. Then Moses says, "Soldiers, Soldiers, cross if you dare!" The remaining children try to get to the other side without being tagged by Moses in the middle. Once everyone is caught, Moses can choose another child as a new Moses.

## 19 Samuel, Samuel!

This game will reinforce the truth of the story of Samuel from 1 Samuel 3. One child is chosen to be "Samuel" and lies down with his back to the group and his eyes closed. The leader then taps one child to say this rhyme:

*"Samuel, Samuel, Can you hear? The Lord your God is always near."*

Samuel then awakens and tries to guess who spoke. When children sit close together it is more challenging to recognize the child speaking. Practice the rhyme several times so that children will be comfortable saying it alone. For younger children the leader might want to simplify the rhyme and simply say, *"Samuel, Samuel, I'm calling you."*

## 20 Creation Memory

This game can be used with the story of creation to talk about all the different kinds of animals God created. Find animal stickers or other duplicate animal pictures. Mount two identical pictures on separate cards. It would be wise to laminate these or cover them with clear contact paper. Using five or six pairs of pictures, depending on the age of the children, play a memory game. Cards are turned over, picture face down. Children take turns turning over two pictures, trying to make a match. If they succeed, they can take another turn. The game continues until all the pairs have been matched.

## 21 Babel Blocks (Genesis 11)

Build "The Tower of Babel," letting the children take turns adding a block. When the tower falls, count to see how many blocks were used. The leader might want to build the foundation for the tower first, allowing the children to add blocks on top of this foundation. Let the children pretend to talk in different languages. They will enjoy having permission to make noise!

## 22 Blinded

After hearing the story of the blind man, in John 9, children may gain greater understanding of the blind while playing this game. Hide some familiar objects in a large bowl or trash can filled with rice and see if the children can identify them simply by touch. You can blindfold them to keep them from peeking.

## 23 Nice Kitty

This story ties in with the story of Daniel in the lions' den (Daniel 6). Have the group stand in a circle with their hands behind their backs. Choose one player to be Daniel and stand in the center of the circle. The leader walks behind the circle and puts a penny in a player's palm; that player is a kitty.

Any player who is not a kitty is a lion. Daniel walks around the circle, approaches a player,

and asks, "Nice kitty?" If a kitty is chosen, the kitty says "Meow," and changes places with Daniel. The leader must now collect and redistribute the pennies. If Daniel chooses a lion, the lion roars, and Daniel must stay in the circle.

## 24 Moses in the Bulrushes (Exodus 2:1-10)

Select one child to be Moses who stands in the center as the other children join hands and walk in a circle around him. To the tune of, "**Farmer in the Dell**," have them sing:

*Moses in the Nile,*
*Watch out for crocodile.*
*All the day bulrushes sway,*
*Moses in the Nile.*
*The princess comes along,*
*The princess comes along,*
*All the day bulrushes sway,*
*Moses in the Nile.*

Moses selects one child to be the princess. The song continues as *"the princess takes a maid," "the maid takes Miriam,"* and *"Miriam takes mother."* The children inside the circle then join the circle and the "mother" gets to play the part of Moses and the song begins again.

## 25 Wooly

Jesus is our Good Shepherd (John 10:1-18). Make two large hand prints on poster board and turn them upside down so the fingers become the legs for a lamb and the thumb is the nose. Spread white glue on the palm section of each hand print. Place cotton balls and a pair of salad tongs at the starting line and the lambs on a table ten feet away. At the "go" signal the first person on each of two teams uses the salad tongs to pick up one cotton ball, carry it to their team's lamb, and place it on the glued area. They then return the tongs to the next teammate who repeats the action. The team that covers their lamb with "wool" first wins.

## 26 Tumbling Walls

Help the children remember the story of the walls of Jericho (Joshua 6:1-27) by playing this game. Divide children into two groups. One group interlocks arms to form the walls of Jericho while the other group marches around "Jericho" seven limes, singing as they go (tune of "Ring Around the Rosie"):

*We're marching around Jericho.*
*Our feet go stomp, our trumpets blow!*
*Praise God!*
*Praise God!*
*The walls fall down!*

The "walls" begin to shake and crumble until all children who are the "wall of Jericho" are on the floor. The children change places and play again.

## 27 Ten Plagues

After studying the plagues of Egypt (Exodus 7-12), play this game so the children can review the story as they work together. Divide the group into teams of five. Assign the name of a different plague to each group, using as many of the ten as you have teams for. Have the children stand around a parachute, holding the edge. (An old sheet will work if a parachute is not available.) Place an inflated beach ball in the center of the parachute. Call the name of one of the plagues and all the children in that group shake the parachute trying to toss the bail off the parachute. In ten or fifteen seconds call a different plague name and then it is that team's turn to try to bounce the bail off the parachute.

## 28 Joseph's coat

After studying Joseph and his colorful coat (Genesis 37:1-4) play this game to help the children appreciate the story. Paint colored stripes on a sheet to resemble Joseph's coat of many colors and spread it out on the floor. Assign a different point value for each colored stripe. Divide the group into two or more teams, or let the children play as individuals. The children will take turns tossing bean bags onto the coat from five feet away to see how many points they can score.

## 29 Feeding the 5,000 (Matthew 14:14-22)

Divide the group into four or more teams. Have a large bowl filled with fish shaped crackers in the center of the activity. Have the teams spaced evenly around the bowl, with the first person on each team standing ten feet away from the bowl. At the "go" signal the first child on each team will run to the bowl, scoop a spoonful of fish crackers, race back, and drop the fish into their team's basket. The teams will race until all children have gone twice. The team with the most fish crackers wins.

## 30 God the Light

Play a version of "Red light, Green light" by the name of "God's the Light." God's the Light = Green Light and Stop All Sin = Red Light. When all the children reach the game leader, count with the children, "1, 2, 3" (to get their attention) then shout in unison "God's The Light!"

## 31 Find It! (Luke 15)

All children sit on the floor in a circle and one child is chosen to be the Searcher. The Searcher turns to face away from the circle while another child is chosen to "hide" the lost coin by sitting on it. Then, the Searcher is invited to walk around the outside of the circle while all the other children sing (to the tune of "Farmer in the Dell"):

*Oh, where is your lost coin?*
*Oh, where is your lost coin?*
*Search until you find it, now.*
*Oh, where is your lost coin?"*

The children sing louder as the Searcher gets closer to the coin and softer as the Searcher moves further away from the coin. The Searcher uses this clue to guess who is hiding the coin and then pats that child on the head.

When the Searcher correctly identifies the child hiding the coin, they exchange places and the child hiding the coin becomes the Searcher. Continue play until everyone has had a chance to be the Searcher.

## 32 Telephone Line to Heaven

Begin by having the children sit in two single-file lines, facing each other. Talk about how the disciples in Acts 1-9 went out and told others the good news about Jesus. Then tell them that each line will receive a message that they must pass on to others, as the disciples did. A leader will whisper the message into the first child's ear and the team must pass the message all the way down the line by whispering the message only once into the next child's ear. The first team to get the message all the way to the end, and have the last person stand and say the message correctly, wins. If neither team gets it correct, the leader can tell everyone the original message and start a new one. Messages should be about the good news of Jesus. ("Jesus died for you!" "Jesus is God's son!" "Jesus is alive!")

## 33 Catching Fish

Four children, called fishermen, hold the corners of an old sheet. When the leader says "GO!" the fishermen raise the sheet and then lower it to the ground while the other kids try to run from one side of the sheet to the other without being trapped underneath. When there are only four fish left uncaught, they become the new fishermen Tell about how Jesus' disciples (in Luke 5) caught more fish than they could hold.

## 34 Active Feet

After teaching the story of the lame man (John 5, Matthew 9, Acts 3), help the children to appreciate their strong legs by playing some relay races. Remind the children frequently that they could not join in if they did not have two strong feet. Sometime during the activity stop and pray, thanking God for healthy bodies.

Suggested relays: Run, jump, hop, gallop, or march to a boundary line and back. Crawl like a spider. Hop with a ball between the legs. Walk on tiptoe.

## 35 The Walls of Jericho (Joshua 6)

For this musical game, have all the kids in the group join hands in a circle. In the center of the circle, two kids should hold the corners of a blanket. The leader sings the song below while the children walk in a circle. Children can join in as they learn the words:

(TUNE: "POP GOES THE WEASEL")

*The walls are high in Je-ri-cho*
*How can we make it over?*
*We asked God to show us the way*
*And this is what He told us.*
*March round 'n' round the city walls*
*March round a count of seven.*
*And when we all began to shout...*
*Crash!*
   (children give a loud clap)
*The walls came tumbling down!*
*"1... 2... 3... 4... 5... 6... 7...*

When the song says "CRASH" the two kids holding the blanket in the center put it on the ground and everyone will rush to find a place to sit down by the count of seven. The last two to be seated on the blanket must hold the blanket for the next round. As the kids become more comfortable with the game and more familiar with the words to the song, encourage them to sing it along with you. The children will also enjoy making the clap on "Crash!" as loud as possible.

# 36 Storm

This group activity can be used to simulate the events of Matthew 8, when Jesus calmed the storm. (This story is also found in Mark 4 and Luke 8.) Place a sheet in an open part of the room. Instruct the children in your group to find a place around the sheet to hold on to. Once everyone has a spot that they can hold onto with both hands, tell the children to drop to their knees and kneel next to the sheet-but don't let go of the sheet. Place a beach ball on the sheet and have children move the "water" (sheet) slowly, watching the "boat" (ball) gently move. Then, make the waves higher by moving the sheet more vigorously with the goal of keeping the ball on the sheet. When the leader whispers, "Jesus said, 'Be still,'" the children stop moving the sheet and make the sea calm again. You can repeat this a number of times, varying the amount of time the kids have to move the water before you instruct them to make it still. Once the children have mastered this activity on their knees, have them try it standing up.

# 37 Colorful Coat Toss-Up

*In advance:* Stuff a paper bag with newspaper or tissue paper, so it is full but not too heavy. Tape the end of the bag securely. Next, take many colors of markers and draw all over the bag, to symbolize the many colors that were in Joseph's coat.

Have the group stand in a circle. Tell the children that the objective of this game is to see how long the group can cooperate and keep the bag in the air by taking turns tossing it up. The kids can move into the circle once the game starts in order to catch the "coat" but encourage them to stay in their own area so that children in all parts of the circle have a chance to play. The children can bump the bag back up into the air if they want to, but it is probably easiest to have the children catch the bag and then throw it back into the air.

Practice this for a while and then have the kids count as a group to see how many times in a row they can throw the bag and catch it without it touching the floor. An optional way to play this is to paint the bag with glow-in-the-dark paints or put glow-in-the-dark tape on it so that you can turn out the lights and have kids play in the dark.

# 38 Noah's Ark (Genesis 6:1-9:1)

Give a feel for what life on Noah's Ark might have been like with this game. Make a masking tape ark shape on the floor. Group the children into pairs and assign a different animal to each pair. Let them sit in the "ark" to listen to the story, giving each animal pair a "stall." After the story is over, have the children think of the sound and motion that their animal pair makes. Then the leader calls the names of the animals. When each pair hears their animal name called, they make their sound and motion. Start off calling out the names slowly so that the children can get used to hearing their animal names and responding. Then start to call the names of the animals faster and faster so they have to listen carefully for their turn to "speak." When one pair of animals forgets to "speak" they leave the ark and sit around the edge of it to help listen for others who might miss their call. Continue playing, giving the animals different instructions for each round. (Instructions could include things such as: make your animal sounds very softly, make your animal motions very large, or very small, etc.) The last animal pair that is left in the "ark" wins the game.

## Bible Times Games

# 39 Fill Up the Jar

Explain to the children that beans and lentils were common foods in Bible times. Place a big container of beans and lentils on the floor and an empty cooking pot a few yards away. Announce that the whole class is going to see how much of the pot they can fill in two minutes. Give each child a small cup and demonstrate how they will scoop the beans into their cup, carry them to the pot, pour them in, and go back for more. Now, set the timer, and let the fun begin!

## 40 Oil for My Lamp

Tell the children about oil lamps that were used for household lighting during Bible times. The children can pretend their paper cups are the lamps, and the water is the oil. Have each child fill their "lamp" half full, and then race from a start to finish line. The winner is the first to get across the line without spilling any water. If anyone spills all of their water, their lamp is out of oil and they must close their eyes and walk in darkness across the finish line. (You may want to spread a tarp or sheet on the floor to catch any spills.)

## 41 Donkey Relay

Discuss with your group that animals were used for transportation in Bible times and it was the rider's responsibility to make sure the animal had food and drink to survive long, hot trips. Divide the group into two equal teams and have each child find a partner. One child begins the race as the donkey, and the other as the rider. When the leader says, "Go!" the donkey, with rider on back, crawls as fast as possible to a plastic pitcher of water at the other side of the room. Here the rider must get off the donkey, fill a portion of a cup with water, serve the water to the donkey, and then get down on all fours. The new rider hops on and the pair races back to the starting point. The rider now gets off the donkey and feeds it a carrot or apple slice, signaling the next pair in line to go. The first team to have everyone finished and seated wins.

## 42 The Lost Sheep

Children sit in a circle with one child, selected to be the shepherd, seated in the middle. While the shepherd's eyes are closed, the leader will give a little piece of wool (cotton ball) to one of the children. Explain that the wool represents a lost sheep and that in Bible times a shepherd watched his sheep carefully to make sure none of them got lost or hurt. Once the wool is safely hidden behind the child's back, the whole group says, "Shepherd, shepherd, where is your sheep?" The shepherd can now look around and guess who has the wool. Once the sheep is found, that child becomes the new shepherd.

## 43 Taking a Trip

Talk with the children about how Jesus and his disciples traveled many places. They didn't have cars or airplanes, so most of the time they walked. Go on a walking journey around the room together by placing cards in a box that have instructions written on them such as, walk to the window, turn around, take two steps backward. All the kids should stand in a group around the leader and take turns drawing a card from the box. The leader reads the card and the whole group follows the instructions together.

## 44 Gone Fishing

Children sit on the floor in a row with hands in back of them. They are fish. One child, chosen to be the fisherman, sits facing the fish. Explain that the fisherman is looking for a treasure (a bag of fish crackers), but the fish are hiding it. The fisherman covers his eyes while the leader places the treasure in the hands of a fish. The fisherman uncovers his eyes when the leader says "PASS!" The treasure is passed from one fish to another (behind their backs) in either direction. The leader says "STOP!" and the passing of the treasure stops. The fisherman tries to name the player who has the bag. At the end, share fish crackers with the children. (Fresh ones may be needed to replace crushed ones from the bag!) While the kids eat, talk about how people who lived in the time of Jesus fished as their job.

## 45 Fishermen

This is a simulation game about the livelihood of fishermen in Bible times.

The leader can arrange two sheets in different areas to represent nets like the ones mentioned in Luke 5:4. The nets trapped fish like a huge bag in the water. Divide the class into two teams and choose one child from each team to throw fish (3" x 5" cards). All the other members of the team must hold the sides of the sheet and work together to catch the fish as they are thrown. Each team then pulls their "fish catch" to an imaginary boat. The team who brings in the most fish wins.

## 46 Pass the Crown

The Bible is full of kings and queens, both good ones who obeyed God and others who did not. For this game the children will pass a crown around the circle from head to head. As long as it is moving, it is the crown of a good king or queen but when the leader rings a bell, the crown stops and the child who has the crown is out. The game continues until only one child is left.

## 47 Journey by Foot

How far have you walked in your life? Well, the Israelites walked for years! In fact, many people in the Bible walked a lot. During this "journey by foot" obstacle course, time the kids and see who can get through it the fastest. Use what you have in the room to make the obstacle course. Some suggestions: crawl under a table, step over shoe boxes, walk through plastic bowling pins without knocking them over, eat a cracker, drink some water, and crawl through a box backward.

## 48 Run, Donkey, Run

Divide the group into teams and have team members pair up. Give each pair a length of yarn or string. At the signal, the first pair each takes an end of the string and stretches it between them. With one as the "front legs" and one as the "back legs," the two children gallop around a chair at the other end of the playing area, then back to the line. When tagged, the next pair can go.

## 49 Carpenter Workshop

Give each team of kids a pile of screws and nuts. Set a timer for two minutes and see how many they can get put together in that amount of time. The team that gets the most wins. Although he didn't use the modern supplies of screws and nuts, Jesus' father was a carpenter. Talk with the kids about ways Jesus might have helped his father in the workshop.

## 50 Into the Fold

Explain to the children that shepherds in the Bible had to protect their sheep. Every night they brought them into the fold where they were protected from wild animals. Play a game of crawling tag where some children kneel together in a semi-circle to make a fold, one child is the wolf, and the others are sheep. The wolf chases the sheep (with everyone down on all fours) but cannot tag any sheep while they are inside the fold.

## 51 Oh, Great King!

In the days of some Bible characters, such as Esther, the kings were very powerful. No one could even see the king unless he allowed it. If you went to see a king without being invited, he could have you killed, unless he extended the end of his golden scepter and accepted you. Play a version of "Mother May I" called, "Oh, Great King." One child, chosen to be the king, stands in front of the group and is given something that represents the golden scepter. Each child in their turn says, "Oh, Great King, may I _____?" (some action, such as take two steps forward). The King says nothing but extends the scepter if that child can take the requested action. If the scepter is not extended, the child cannot move on that turn.

## 52 Sheep, Sheep, Shepherd

The Bible is full of stories about sheep and shepherds! Have the children play a variation on "Duck, Duck, Goose." Play just like the original game, except have the children say, "Sheep, Sheep, Shepherd!"

## 53 Battle of the Cotton Balls

During the times recorded in the Old Testament, there were many great battles in which God protected and gave victory to His people. Have the children participate in their own battle with cotton balls. Divide the children into two teams and assign them to opposite sides of the room. Mark a middle line on the floor with masking tape. Distribute cotton balls to each child and tell them that they are to throw the cotton balls across the line, trying to hit a member of the other team. They may go as close to the middle line as they like but cannot cross it. Children should keep track of how many of their own cotton balls strike the enemy, but a child is not out if he or she is hit. Cotton balls that are thrown can be picked up and used again.

## Family Fun Games

## 54 Favorite Family Fun

Rehearse with the children ideas of fun family activities, such as picnicking or hiking. After the children share some of their own ideas, tell the children they get to act out the activity ideas any way they wish to when the leader calls out one of the suggestions. For instance, if the leader calls out "horseback riding!" the children can pretend to climb on a horse, brush a horse, feed a carrot to a horse, etc. If the leader calls out "Family freeze!" all the children should freeze right in their tracks; children who move during the freeze time are out.

## 55 Helpers at Home

*In advance:* In two separate areas, scatter an even number of children's books and toys. Divide the class into two teams. Tell the children that once the leader says to go, they should all work together to 1) stack the books in one cardboard box, 2) stack the toys in the other cardboard box, 3) have all their team members sit down around their team's boxes. Let the children know that even if their team isn't the fastest in the game, they can still help their family at home by picking up their toys.

## 56 Busy Families

This game is similar to "Squirrels in the Trees" and may help children to appreciate the work their parents do for them. Divide children into groups of three. In each group designate one to be the mother, one the father, and the third the baby. The mother and father join hands to form a house. The baby sits inside the house. The leader will call out sentences such as, "Father cuts the grass," "Mother goes to work," "Mother washes our clothes," "Father cooks our meals," "Baby crawls away." Each time mother, father, or baby is mentioned, they exchange places with another mother, father, or baby. If there are one or two extra children, they can be babies also. Several families can have twins!

## 57 Family Circle

This game helps children identify the roles of boys and girls in families as brothers, sisters, mothers and fathers. Instruct children to sit in a circle. Choose one child to walk around the outside of the circle tapping each child on the head. The child says "sister" each time a girl is tapped and "brother" each time a boy is tapped until he chooses someone to chase him around the circle by yelling "Mom!" or "Dad!" This mom or dad chases the child around the circle and back to the original starting point. Then the child joins the Family Circle and the mom/dad becomes the child who taps the other kids in the circle.

## 58 Food Tour

Children follow the leader on an imaginary tour based on something that people in their family do for them. The leader and children can make the motions together. Ideas for tours could include chores around the house or going to work. A tour of the grocery store where parents shop for food might go something like this:

"Let's take a tour of the grocery store to see some of the wonderful foods our parents make for us. Brr! When the door opens, feel that air conditioning. (Shiver, shiver.) The manager of the store said we could sample anything we like. Yum! Yum! (Rub stomach.) Let's start here in the fruits and vegetables. Mmm. Here's a ripe banana. (Peel and eat banana.) Here's some crunchy celery. (Fake a big crunchy bite.) Hey! I love corn on the cob, don't you? (Eat corn.) God sure thought of a lot of interesting foods. Isn't it wonderful that we have parents who buy and prepare our food, and families to eat with? What foods do you see?"

## 59 Family Statues

Play some music while the kids act out their favorite activity to do with their family. When the music stops, all the children freeze. The leader then tries to guess what different children are doing. After guessing a few, turn the music back on and continue with the game, guessing activities of different children each time.

## 60 Family Sand Sketch

Fill disposable aluminum pie pans with sand and water. Have the children sit on a tarp and give each child one pan. Ask them to use their fingers to sketch a picture in the sand of a member of their family. Then ask the children to erase their pictures by running their hands over the sand. Continue in this way, giving the children things to sketch in the sand. Include things such as different members of their family, their pets, their house, their yard, their favorite toy, etc. For variety, divide the children into pairs or have them choose partners. Each child's partner must try to guess what the other child is sketching in his or her sand. The children can alternate sketching and guessing with their partners.

## 61 Gather the Family

On several index cards, draw stick figures to represent members of the family. (Skirt on mom, tie on dad,)ponytails for girl, short hair for boy, baby, grandpa with beard, grandma with bun in hair.) Make enough of each card that the children can have one for each person in their real family. Show the cards to the children and explain to them what family member each card stands for. Place the cards in various boxes around the room. Have at least one box for each different family member card. At the signal, each child must gather a card for each member in their family. Make sure that the children know that their card collection will not be the same as others because everyone's families are different. Once the children have collected a card that represents each person in their family, they should sit down and raise their cards in the air. Once all the children are finished, take volunteers to come to the front of the group to show their cards and tell the names of the people in their family. Have some extra cards on hand in case a child is missing a card when they describe their family to the group.

## 62 Baby Games

This game helps to build appreciation for babies and understanding of what is involved for a family to take care of one. Set up a circle of chairs in advance and make small signs to tape to most of the chairs. Each sign should have a symbol related to baby care. For example, draw a rubber duck for bath time, or a rattle for play time, a bottle for meals, or a diaper for changing time. Tell the children to walk around the circle and then sit in a chair as soon as they hear the leader say "BABY." If the chair they sit in has a symbol on it, the children can act it out. Those children who do not have symbols attached to their chairs can act out a baby crawling. The children should walk (or crawl) around the circle, acting out their symbol until they hear the leader say "BABY" again. When they hear this, they should go to a new chair and sit in it. Now they will have new symbols to act out for this round. Because no one gets out in this game, there should be enough chairs for all the children on each round. When you are finished playing this game, let the children tell their own experiences with babies and why they think babies are special.

# 63 Family wrap

Divide the children into groups of five. Give each group one roll of toilet paper to work with. Instruct the kids that they are to make costumes out of the toilet paper to dress three kids in their group. They must dress these three people in their group to look like a mother, a father, and a son or a daughter. When the children have finished creating their toilet paper costumes, allow each team to model their family for the whole group and explain what costumes they created with the toilet paper. They can also explain why they think it makes the child look like the member of the family that he or she represents. If you have more time, let the children switch places so that the kids who designed the clothes last time get to be dressed up. Assign different family members (aunts, uncles, grandparents, etc.) this time and let the children model the new outfits when they are completed.

# 64 Church-Time Fun

Divide the class into three teams. During this relay race, have the children carry a penny in a paper cup and sit down in a chair halfway to the finish line. While seated in the chair, have the children sing the chorus of "Jesus Loves Me," and run the distance from the chair to the finish line. Finally, they can deposit a penny in a box to simulate an offering collection and then run back to their teammates. Have each child take turns repeating the same actions until each child has finished. See which team is done first.

# 65 Bible Puzzle Hunt

Reading and learning Bible verses is an important part of going to church, and this is a fun way to do it! Write out a verse putting only one word on each index card. Place the cards end to end and cut matching shapes so the cards fit together like a puzzle. Hide the cards around the room and let the children search for them. Once they have all the cards they can all work to fit the puzzle pieces together. Once the puzzle is complete, have a leader read the verse out loud and the kids repeat it.

# 66 Musical Prayer

Write numbers on masking tape and place them on the floor in a circle. Each child stands on a number and then the whole group moves around the circle while singing, "Jesus Loves Me." At the end of the song each child should be standing on a new number. The leader then calls out a number and that child shares one thing he or she is thankful for. After a few children have shared, the leader will say a prayer thanking God for the things mentioned. Repeat as many times as desired!

## 67 Popcorn

Children will find that reviewing Bible verses in church is fun with the following activity: Children may sit in a circle or a straight line. Designate one child to begin the Bible verse by "popping up" and saying the first word. The next child "pops up" with the second word. Each child continues with the next word. Repeat the verse until all have had an opportunity to participate. Afterwards, reward them with a popcorn treat.

## 68 Going to Church

Help kids make up motions to this fun song (to the tune of *Here We Go 'Round the Mulberry Bush*) as they learn to understand and appreciate their time in church.

Suggested verses:
***This is the way we go to church,***
***Go to church, go to church,***
***This is the way we go to church,***
***On a Sunday morning.***

***This is the way we greet our friends.***
***This is the way we read God's word.***
***This is the way we close our eyes.***
***This is the way we say our prayers.***
***This is the way we give our gifts.***
***This is the way we listen well.***
***This is the way we sing to God.***
***This is the way we say good bye.***

## 69 Musical Plates

Begin the game by puffing a paper plate on the floor for each child. Turn on some Bible songs that the kids will enjoy hearing and learning. Instruct the children to move, sing, and clap. When the music stops, each child should walk to a plate and stand on it. When the music begins again, the children should leave their plates and return to what they were doing. Continue to play like musical chairs, removing one plate each time. The kids who are "out" can still enjoy the music and can help the leader by choosing which plates to take out.

## 70 Boom, Boom, Clang, Clang

One important way of praising God in church is through music. Sometimes music makes you want to jump, shout, and sing! Create a joyful band to make music for God by giving the children various instruments (or let kids make the instrument sounds themselves). The leader conducts a parade around the room, weaving here and there and calling out the names of instruments. Children with those instruments join the parade and start making a joyful noise to the Lord. The leader can also give instructions to skip, jump, and spin around.

## 71 The Working Church

Everyone in the church is important and has special talents and jobs. Help the kids see some of the different people in the church and how important each person is by acting out these roles of people in the church. Have the kids repeat the actions and words after the leader. When you finish acting out all the roles, see if the kids can think of any other people in the church. Help the kids make up actions to show what their jobs are.

Pastor: (holding an imaginary book) ***"This is what the Bible says."***

Choir member: (sings) ***"la-la-la!"***

Janitor: (singing and sweeping) ***"This is the way we sweep the church.".***

Receptionist: (answering a phone) ***"Hello, may I help you?"***

Kid: (singing) ***"Jesus loves me, this I know."***

Nursery worker: (cradling an imaginary baby) ***"There, there, little baby."***

Sunday school teacher: (opening an imaginary Bible) ***"Who knows today's memory verse?"***

Music director/choir leader: (opens an imaginary song book) ***"Let's all praise God together,"***

## 72 Going to Church

Going to church can be a fun thing to do... especially with a friend. Choose two children to form the church door by clasping hands and raising their arms. All the other children move single file through the door as they sing (to the tune of "**London Bridge**"):

*How I love to go to church,*
*Go to church, go to church.*
*How I love to go to church.*
*Won't you come with me?*

When the song ends, the two children forming the church door drop their arms and trap the child standing between them. The child caught standing in the "door" when the song ends then chooses a partner to form a new door. Once the new church door is in place, the children begin walking through it, singing the song, and the whole game repeats.

## 73 Stop the music

Describe to the children the many kinds of movement they can make about the church (see below). While the music is playing, have children move about without touching each other. But when the music stops have them "Freeze" in their spots. Let each child tell you what they are doing. Then, start the music again!

(Suggested movement themes:)

Singing hymns or praise songs

Praying

Reading the Bible

Directing the choir

Preaching or teaching

## 74 Take It to the Box

*In advance:* Make slips of paper that are designed to look like dollar bills. You may want to make them resemble different bills or just design them to look like play paper money in general. Hide these slips of paper money around the room. Show the children an example of the paper money. Tell the children that they will be playing a game that has to do with offering bringing our money to God. Tell the kids that you have hidden paper money (like the piece you are holding) around the room. They will have a certain amount of time and in that time they are to try to find as much money as possible. When all the bills are found or when time is up, have the children bring their bills to the front of the room and put them in an offering box. Make sure that every child has something to put in the box. (You may need to have a few spare "bills" in case some of the children don't find any on their own.) To play again, choose a couple of kids to help you hide the "money" and then have the rest of the group begin the search again.

## 75 Church Formation

Divide the children into two teams. Instruct them to build a church building out of their own bodies. The children should work together to figure out what the building should look like and decide how they can fit all their team members together to form that shape. Then they should all lie down on the floor so that their whole team forms the shape of a church building. For younger children, you may want to bring in a simple line-drawing of a church so they have an idea of what their formation should look like. They may also need the help of an adult to visualize what the finished church should look like and to help them decide who should go where. Be available to help the kids but try to let them figure it out on their own first. The important thing is that they get involved and have fun, not that they create a perfect finished product! Remind the kids that even though real church buildings are usually made out of bricks, wood, or stone, the church really is the people!

## Character Building Games

### 76 Let Your Light Shine

This small group game gets children working together using flashlights, symbolizing the light we share as Christians. Before the game begins, make two large circles on the floor with masking tape. Give each child a flashlight. Break the group up into two small teams. Explain that each team should try to focus their individual flashlight beam with the others on their team so the combined flashlights make one large light. (You may need to demonstrate.) Tell the children that the first team to focus their lights together and trace their circle on the floor with the combined beam, wins.

### 77 Strong and Courageous

We often have to do things that we are scared of but God can help us have the courage to do them. David is a good example of courage as he faced the lions and bears to protect his father's sheep (1 Samuel 17:33-37). Emphasize the fact that it was only with the Lord's help that David had the courage to do what he did. In this game, based on the courage that David showed, have the children line up and take turns throwing a table tennis ball, with sticky Velcro strips on it, at a felt picture of a lion or a bear. Cheer for the children as they try to protect their sheep from these animals.

### 78 Friends Help Each Other

This game focuses on the concept of friends helping each other. Select pairs of children to work as partners and give each pair a heart cut out of red construction paper. Explain to the children that they both need to hold onto the paper heart, start out from the common starting line, and try to be the first pair to go across the finish line with their paper heart still intact. They must help each other to move quickly without tearing the heart. (But if everyone tears their heart, find out which child's heart is torn the least.)

### 79 Let's Work Together

Bring in various objects that come in pairs and have the group identify them together. (Examples: sock and shoe, plate and napkin, crayon and paper, book and bookmark, etc.) Then take the objects and scatter them throughout the room. Each child should find a partner and hold a paper bag between the two of them. Then they must walk together around the room and find pairs of objects that go together. Each child must pick up one of the objects and when both are found, they can put them in the bag together. The first partners to find three pairs of objects yell, "Friends!" Those children sit down until the other partners have found three pairs of objects or all the objects have been collected. Talk about how each set of partners had to work together and how working together can help us be better friends.

### 80 Blind Thankfulness

Have half the kids create a maze by crouching down to become rocks to go around, forming arches with their arms to go under, and kneeling with their arms extended to make logs to step over. Have the other half of the group pair off with one partner being blind and the other the leader. Have the partners go all the way through the maze and then switch places. The goal is not to be the fastest but to lead your partner safely through the maze. How thankful we should be for the friends that help us and for good eyes that can see!

### 81 Air Bag

Mark a starting line and a finish line on the floor using masking tape. Give each child a table-tennis ball and have kids line up behind the starting line. Explain to the children that they should place their ball on the floor, kneel behind their ball, then gently blow it toward the finish line. Play against the clock, with children playing several times and trying to beat their previous time record. Talk about the importance of perseverance and sticking with something even when it is hard.

# 82 Hug Parade

This version of "London Bridge" gives children a chance to show God's love to others. Have one child join hands with you to create an arch. Have the other children parade under the arch as you sing this song to the tune of *London Bridge*.

*God wants us to show our love,*
*Show our love,*
*Show our love.*
*God wants us to show our love,*
*To each other.*

On the word "other," drop your arms around the child who is under the arch. Together with the child holding your hands, hug the child in the middle. Then let this child join hands with you to create the arch and play again. Continue playing until each child has been hugged at least once!

# 83 Wonderfully Made

To encourage self esteem and to teach the truth of Psalm 139:14. ("I am... wonderfully made.") introduce the following game: Children stand in a circle and one child begins by saying, "I am wonderfully made. I can ___. He fills in the blank with such words as "jump," "laugh," or "crawl." The rest of the children join in doing what the child says. Go around the circle, allowing each child to have a turn. At the end, see if the group can name all of the activities and do them in order.

# 84 Heaped in a Hoop

Begin by laying some large plastic hoops around the room. (Start with one for each child if possible. Otherwise assign a certain number of children who can be in a hoop to begin with.) Play some music and have the children walk around the hoops, but tell them not to touch any of them while the music is playing. When the music stops, each child steps into the nearest hoop. There should be enough hoops for every child. Once everyone has found a hoop, the leader chooses a hoop to take out of play. The leader removes the hoop and then starts the music again. The game continues as before and each time the music stops, children must step into the nearest hoop. No one is ever out in this game because as hoops are removed, there can be more than one child in each hoop. Play until there are only one or two hoops left. Encourage the kids to help each other find room for every child inside these two hoops. It is quite crowded with all those kids heaped in a hoop-but fun too! Then, without music, see if you can fit everyone in your group into one hoop.

# 85 Finders Keepers

This game helps children develop good teamwork skills. Divide the group into teams. Have each team choose a "finder." Together (with a leader), the players and finders determine a special call they will use to identify themselves: perhaps a "beep" or a "clap" or an "eek!" Calls should only be one syllable. Once each team's call is decided, the finders turn their backs or leave the room while all the other players hide. When the finders return, have all the lights turned off. At the signal, the finders try to find their fellow team members by listening for the special calls. The children who are hiding should try to make it easy to be found by repeating their team's special call over and over again. When a finder locates a person on his or her team, the finder places his or her hand on the child's head and makes the team's special call. The child who has been found answers with the call and then goes to sit in a designated area for that team. If the child is from a different team and answers with a different call, the finder should leave that child alone and go on to find someone from his or her own team. The first team to have everyone found by the finder and to be seated all together in their area wins.

## 86 Who Got My Boots?

Divide the group into teams. Put enough pairs of shoes and boots in a pile so there is one pair for each child. At the signal, the first child in each line runs to the pile and tries to find a matching pair of shoes. Children remove their own shoes and add them to the pile, then put on the new pair and run to tag the next child in line. The first team to have all players back in line in new shoes wins, but continue the game until all team members on all teams have played. Now play again—the object being that everyone finds their own shoes. No one can win on their own—the whole team must work together to win!

## 87 Gentleness Grab Bag

Place a number of objects that have to be handled with gentleness into paper bags. Items could include an egg, a water balloon, a baby doll, etc. Have children take turns coming up and putting their hands inside the bags. Without seeing what is inside, see if they can guess what the objects are. To make this a competitive game, divide the kids into teams and see which team can correctly identify the most objects.

## 88 Cooperation

Have each child select a partner and then divide the group into four teams. Assign each team a color-this will be the color of their team's balloons. The first set of partners on each team will be given one table-tennis paddle each. Place a balloon between the paddles. Each partner must put enough pressure on the paddle to secure the balloon long enough to carry it to a box ten feet away. When the partners have successfully placed their balloon in the box, they run back, give the paddles to the next set of partners on their team, and play continues. If a pair drops a balloon, they are disqualified, and they must take the paddles to the next pair in line. When everyone else has gone, the pairs that dropped their balloons get one more chance to take their balloon to the box. The team that has the most balloons in the box when all teams have completed the exercise is the winner.

## 89 Pass It on!

Divide the class in half and seat them on the floor in two circles, back to back (one facing in and the other facing out). Instruct each circle to pass a ball or bean bag around the circle as they sing (to the tune of *Mary Had a Little Lamb*):

*I know Jesus loves us so,*
*Loves us so, loves us so.*
*I know Jesus loves us so,*
*And I will pass it on!*

Each time the verse ends, the two children holding the ball or bean bag exchange places.

# Happy Holiday Games

## 90 Christmas Angel Action

The excitement of Jesus' birth can be relived through remembering the host of angels which heralded the occasion. Play a version of "Pin the Tail on the Donkey." Have the children pin angel pictures on top of a picture of a Christmas tree.

## 91 Fill the Manger

Have three teams of children line up behind starting marks. Explain what a manger is and that a manger was Jesus' first bed. Tell the children that each team is responsible for transporting the straw (or shredded paper) to their team's box, simulating the real manger Jesus slept in. The first team that can successfully transport every piece of straw or paper to fill their box wins the competition.

## 92 Hide the Easter Eggs

This game helps children to learn a Bible verse related to Easter. Write out the Bible verse Matthew 28:20, ". . . I, Jesus, am with you always..." (one word for each piece of paper.)

Associate each word with an illustration from a pictorial sequence of a flower growing (ground, seed, sprout, bud, leaf, flower). Insert each word in a plastic egg. Each team will have the same verse hidden in their team's eggs and each team's eggs will be a different color. The leader hides the eggs for each team. The team that can find all the eggs, unscramble the verse, and put the verse together in correct order according to the plant sequence pictures, wins. Since the children won't be able to read, they will put it together according to the flower pictures and then a leader can read the verse at the end.

## 93 Follow the Star

This game goes with the story of the Wise Men who followed the star of Bethlehem. Cut out star shapes from the two different colors of construction paper. Tape the stars (at least twenty for each team) around an area for children to find them. Divide the class into teams. Assign one of the star colors to each team. Set the timer for one minute. Explain to the children that the team that finds the most stars for their team during the time limit wins. Hide the stars in new places and play again.

## 94 Secret Picture Card Game

Use this game to review or tell the Easter story. Divide the children into groups of two to three and give each group one card. The cards should each have a picture of something that relates to the story (three crosses, the large rock in front of the tomb, an angel, etc.) Once the groups have their card, let them talk together to make sure they all agree on what it is. Then one member from each group comes to the front and holds the card so the rest cannot see it. The large group tries to guess what the secret picture is by asking yes or no questions. Once all the cards have been guessed, have the group work together to put them in order of how the story really happened.

## 95 Candy Canes

Use this game to bring significance to a Christmas symbol. Tell the children this candy cane story: It was first made by a candy maker in England many years ago. He wanted children to think about Jesus' birthday so he made the candy cane as a reminder. The three red stripes remind us of the Father, Son, and Holy Spirit. The wider stripe stands for Jesus. White is for His purity, red for His blood. It looks like a shepherd's staff. Upside down, it is a "J." Hide candy canes in the room and let the children hunt for them. If you have a tree in the room, the children can add some as decorations.

## 96 Musical Hearts

This game may be used for Valentine's Day as a reminder of God's love. This game is a reversed version of "Musical Chairs." Place two hearts cut from poster board on the floor in a large circle. Write "God is love" or "Jesus loves me" on each heart. Begin with one child walking around the hearts while the music play. When the music stops, that child stands on a heart and any other child can go and stand on the second heart. Add a heart each time until all the children are standing on hearts. Talk with the kids about how God's love is big enough for all of us.

# 97 Holiday Hustle

This game uses good listening skills and helps kids learn certain things that are associated with Christian holidays. Establish two boundary lines (indoors or outdoors) far enough apart so that children can run from one to the other. Have the children line up on one boundary line. The leader should stand behind the children and the boundary line. The leader tells the children what holiday name to listen for, such as Easter. The leader calls out words of things that are typically associated with that holiday (empty tomb, cross, new life, stone rolled away). The children should stay on the boundary line until they hear the leader say the actual holiday name. When the holiday name is called the children run to the other boundary and the leader chases them. Any children who are caught must freeze and stand where they were tagged. They must stand there frozen until they hear the leader call the name of the next holiday. The child can then run from his or her frozen spot to the boundary line that the other children are running toward. It's best to do mostly chasing with just enough catching to make it a fun and exciting challenge for the kids.

# 98 Holiday Bowling

Decorate (or have the children decorate) some plastic or paper cups for whatever holiday you are celebrating. You may want to use stickers and already made holiday pictures or let the children simply color the cups with colors that are associated with a particular holiday (green and red for Christmas, pastels for Easter, etc.). Mark a fairly wide bowling lane on the floor using masking tape. On the floor, at the very end of the bowling lane, set up the decorated holiday cups in a formation like bowling pins. Then let the children use a tennis ball or soft indoor ball to bowl. Let the children rotate, taking turns knocking over the cups and setting them up again for the next player. You can designate stations so that there is always one child bowling, one child setting up the pins and one child who is in charge of retrieving the ball and returning it to the next child in line to bowl. If you have a large group, set up more than one bowling lane so that the children can be an active part of holiday bowling the whole time.

# 99 Holiday Concentration

Draw holiday symbols on 3" x 5" index cards. Be sure there are two identical cards of each symbol. Lay the cards upside down, in rows, on the floor. Play a memory game where the children take turns trying to turn over two cards that match. The first child turns over two cards. If they match, he or she gets to keep them and that child gets to choose two cards to turn over again. If the two cards do not match, that child must turn both cards back over and the next child gets to take a turn. The children can only turn over two cards each time, and the child with the most pairs at the end is the winner!

# 100 Snowman Race

Have each child make a snowman out of marshmallows, following these instructions: Use a toothpick as the center for the bodies and stick it through the middle of two large marshmallows. Then stick a toothpick out either side of the top marshmallow of the snowman and attach small marshmallows to the toothpicks to form arms. Let the children draw faces on their marshmallow snowmen using fine tipped markers. Then have a snow-man race! Place some books under two cookie sheets to prop them up side-by-side. They should be the same size and should slope down at the same angle. The angle should be fairly steep so that the snowmen will slide down without getting stuck. Have the children form two lines behind the cookie sheets. As each child gets to the "sledding hills" he or she will place the snowman at the top of the "hill." The child must wait for the snowman from the child in the other line to be ready and then the leader says, "Go!" The two chil-dren then let go of their snowmen and see which makes it to the bottom of the hill first. After everyone has had a chance to race their snowman once, have the winners from each pair line up. Divide them into two lines and have them stand behind the cookie sheet hills. Repeat the racing process for these snowmen. Continue racing the winners of each pair until you have a final race with the winner being the grand champion snowman!